Bill Bright

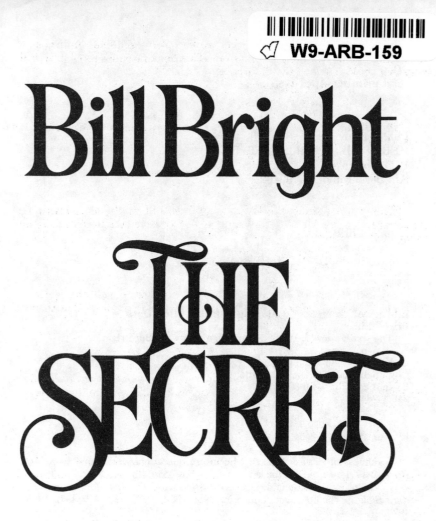

The Secret

Here's Life Publishers

First printing, April 1989

Published by
HERE'S LIFE PUBLISHERS, INC.
P. O. Box 1576
San Bernardino, CA 92402

Library of Congress Cataloging-in-Publication Data
Bright, Bill.
   The secret : how to live with purpose and power / Bill Bright.
      p.   cm.
   ISBN 0-89840-243-3 (pbk.)
   1. Spiritual life.   I. Title.
BV4501.2.B725   1989
248.4 – dc 19   89-30950
                                                           CIP

Unless otherwise indicated, Scripture quotations are from *The Living Bible,* © 1971 by Tyndale House Publishers, Wheaton, Illinois.

Scripture quotations designated NAS are from *The New American Standard Bible,* © The Lockman Foundation 1960, 1962, 1963, 1968, 1971, 1972, 1975, 1977.

Scripture quotations designated NIV are from *The Holy Bible, New International Version,* © 1978 by the New York International Bible Society, published by the Zondervan Corporation, Grand Rapids, Michigan.

Scripture quotations designated KJV are from the *King James Version* of the Bible.

For More Information, Write:
L.I.F.E. – P.O. Box A399, Sydney South 2000, Australia
Campus Crusade for Christ of Canada – Box 300, Vancouver, B.C., V6C 2X3, Canada
Campus Crusade for Christ – Pearl Assurance House, 4 Temple Row, Birmingham, B2 5HG, England
Lay Institute for Evangelism – P.O. Box 8786, Auckland 3, New Zealand
Campus Crusade for Christ – P.O. Box 240, Colombo Court Post Office, Singapore 9117
Great Commission Movement of Nigeria – P.O. Box 500, Jos, Plateau State Nigeria, West Africa
Campus Crusade for Christ International – Arrowhead Springs, San Bernardino, CA 92414, U.S.A.

To Vonette,
my sweetheart and beloved wife,
with whom it has been my delight
to share the adventure
of Spirit-filled marriage and ministry
for four glorious decades.

Also by Bill Bright

Witnessing Without Fear
(Winner of the 1988 Gold Medallion Award)

Promises: A Daily Guide to Supernatural Living

Have You Heard of the Four Spiritual Laws?

Would You Like to Know God Personally?

Have You Made the Wonderful Discovery
of the Spirit-filled Life?

Kingdoms at War

A Handbook for Christian Maturity

The Holy Spirit: Key to Supernatural Living

The Transferable Concepts

Transferable Concepts for Powerful Living

Ten Basic Steps to Christian Maturity

Five Steps to Christian Growth

Come Help Change the World

Revolution Now!

Acknowledgments

Through the years I have written several books and hundreds of articles. There once was a time when my schedule allowed me to personally write, edit and polish each manuscript; today, however, the responsibilities of leading a large worldwide movement and my appointment and travel schedule do not allow me such luxury.

So when God placed a great desire in my heart to write this book, *The Secret,* I happily sought the counsel of my long-time friend, Dan Benson, the editorial director of Here's Life Publishers.

Dan has helped me put into this book the essence of what I have taught and sought to live for approximately four decades. I am indebted to him for his professional assistance in preparing this manuscript.

I also thank Don Tanner, who made pertinent suggestions along the way and joined Dan and me in the editing process.

Contents

You can know without a doubt that
all is right between you and God.

1

Discover
the Secret

If we could but show the world that being com-
mitted to Christ is no tame, humdrum, sheltered
monotony, but the most exciting adventure the human
spirit can ever know, those who have been standing
outside the church and looking askance at Christ
will come crowding in to pay allegiance . . . and
we may well expect the greatest revival since
Pentecost.

James Stewart

How would you like to discover a new dimension of hap-piness and joy in your Christian life?

How would you like to exit the roller coaster ride of spiritual highs and lows . . . and discover a lifestyle of consistent victory?

When you became a Christian, you may have thought that receiving Christ would be the end to your problems. That you would now win over temptation and sin, experience moment-by-moment happiness, handle life's hassles with ease.

But it wasn't that easy, was it? You discovered that a large number of Christians experience spiritual drought. You found that God gives Christians the power of choice, and that we don't always make the right choices. You discovered that God often allows trials to enter our lives, and we don't always respond in ways that honor Him.

Tragically, many believers are trapped on a roller coaster that ascends to great heights and plummets to disheartening lows. Others are wandering a dry wilderness of spiritual lethargy, a far cry from the wellsprings of abundance our Lord Jesus Christ promised to all who trust and obey Him.

Has He broken His promise? Of course not. Instead, these well-meaning Christians have failed to utilize the very source of power Jesus Christ sent to do His work in us. They have not tapped into the Christian's secret to a consistent life.

How about you? Have you recently felt far from God?

Is your sense of inner peace less than it should be?

Have you left your first love for Him?

Are you struggling with sin?

Do you have little desire to read God's Word?

Do you have trouble loving someone—or yourself?

Has prayer become a meaningless experience in your life?

Are you in bondage to a bad habit?

Do you have little interest in sharing Christ with others?

Does your happiness depend on your circumstances?

You are about to discover how you can avoid those

plunges into spiritual lows, how to overcome those long spiritual dry spells. No matter what trials or temptations come your way, whether you're full of energy or in need of forty-eight hours' sleep, you can know without a doubt that all is right between you and God . . . and your life can be a shining example of the love, joy, peace, patience, kindness, goodness, faithfulness, gentleness and self-control He promises.

Off the Fence at Last

Frank, a successful publishing executive, had received Christ as his personal Savior when he was nine. He was raised in a fine Christian home, and had been involved in church activities since early childhood. "But I always rode the fence when it came to Christian commitment," he says. "I didn't do the earth-shaking sins that my friends may have done, but I often was more interested in being 'cool' than in being a positive example of Christianity.

"Frequently, I would experience discouragement and defeat. From reading the Bible and observing my parents and other mature Christians, I had a glimpse of the type of consistency I should have in my life. But I gave in too easily to lustful thoughts, cynicism and spiritual complacency, then would feel guilty and spiritually dead for weeks and months until the next altar call in church—when I would go forward to recommit my life to Christ for the nth time.

"Soon, though, the emotional high of those moments of recommitment would give way to more compromise, and the cycle would start all over again. It was an up-and-down roller coaster ride—mostly down. I just didn't have the happiness and victory Christians are supposed to have."

Then Frank discovered the secret. He attended one of our Christian training conferences where I shared about the ministry of God's Holy Spirit in the life of the believer.

Frank learned that God sent the Holy Spirit to be our personal Comforter, Helper, Teacher and Guide. He learned that he could draw on the strength of the Holy Spirit to help him resist temptation. He learned how to deal with unconfessed sin and live as God wanted Him to live.

"Learning about the personal ministry of the Holy Spirit completely changed my life," Frank reports. "I had been resisting a total commitment to the Lord because I wanted to be dynamic and happy — and ironically, I found that both of these qualities came naturally when I allowed the Holy Spirit to do His job.

"It's great to be off the emotional roller coaster and have greater consistency in my walk with the Lord Jesus. Of course there are still times when I blow it, or feel discouraged or defeated, but now I know how to overcome the dry spells through the resources God has provided. What a difference!"

A Breath of Fresh Air

JoAnne, who received Christ at age twelve, determined that she was going to "be a good Christian if it kills me." And with white knuckles and clenched teeth she did everything she knew good Christians are supposed to do: she "went to Sunday school and church, didn't smoke or drink, watched Billy Graham on TV and tried to be nice to my older sister."

But at age twenty-one, after nine years of defeat, frustration and guilt, JoAnne realized "something was wrong. I concluded I must not be a Christian. After all, if I were a Christian, why couldn't I act like one?"

JoAnne was attending the University of Nebraska when she was invited to a Leadership Training Conference sponsored by Campus Crusade for Christ. "There, I heard for the first time that the Christian life is not a bunch of do's and don'ts—rather, it is a moment-by-moment walk with God that depends on *His* power to give me the strength to live a successful Christian life.

"Almost immediately I began to experience the freedom of allowing God's Holy Spirit to work in me. What a breath of fresh air it was to realize that I didn't have to struggle and strain to live the Christian life in my own efforts!"

JoAnne's discovery was thirteen years ago. Now a personnel administrator, she continues to enjoy the stability and strength that comes from allowing the Holy Spirit to empower and guide her life.

Able to Forgive Father

For Stacy, the struggle was with the deep hurt she felt toward her father. "For years he had shown hatred toward my mother and me with violence and constant criticism," Stacy says. "Bitterness ruled every ounce of my being, and nothing would have given me greater pleasure than to see him suffer for the hurt he had caused us. Forgiving him was the last thing I wanted to, or could, do."

Then Stacy became involved with a group of fellow Christians in a study of the ministry of the Holy Spirit in the life of the believer. As she learned how to tap into the power available to her, she gradually began to sense a change in attitude toward her father and people in general. "I was filled with more and more of God's supernatural love," she recalls, "and my bitterness faded until I finally was able to forgive my dad and others who had hurt me.

"I couldn't do it on my own. I needed the special love only God can provide—and He did! It is as though God has placed His heart of compassion in me, so now I can honestly say that I love my dad, and others as well. God has completely changed a situation that I thought was hopeless and

I was powerless to change."

Power to Live the Christian Life

Andrew is a sharp, dedicated high school senior who provides leadership to his church youth group. Through the influence of his parents and a good church, Andrew received Christ as a young boy. Yet, he reports, "like many of the elders' kids I was a 'good little boy' but experienced little spiritual growth. In the summer of 1984 I rededicated my life to Christ, but still felt that something was missing.

Andrew realizes now that living the Christian life is not only difficult—it is impossible. Without the power of God's Holy Spirit within us, we cannot possibly have the strength to resist temptation and make the right choices. "The message had never reached me that I must let the Lord, in the form of the Holy Spirit, live the Christian life through me," he says. "I cannot express the joy I felt when I discovered that the 'burden' of living the Christian life is really no burden at all—because the Holy Spirit will live it through me if I invite Him and trust Him to do so."

Freedom From Sexual Guilt

John, an elder in the church, was a good-looking, decent family man. He could always be counted on to help others or listen to their problems. But when things at the office got a little hectic, John began to forsake his regular times of study and reflection in God's Word. His prayer life suffered. As a result, spiritual priorities took a back seat. He did not feel as intimate with his wife as he once did, and he started to fear that the years were passing by too quickly.

So John was primed for the fall when Sabrina, an attractive young co-worker, appeared at his office door in tears one evening after work.

Sabrina was having trouble with her self-image. Her fiancé had just broken their engagement, and she felt used, unwanted, unattractive. John was quick to assure Sabrina that she was still extremely attractive. As one after-hours counseling session led to another, John and Sabrina found themselves embroiled in a series of secret sexual encounters.

At first, John rationalized his behavior: His wife didn't understand him; knowing that a younger woman desired him helped him "feel young" again. But the momentary pleasures of the affair soon gave way to dark clouds of guilt. He loved his wife and family. What had fleetingly made him feel more important was now showing him how low he could stoop. He could not bear the guilt that was overwhelming him.

That's where John stood when he learned how the Holy Spirit wanted to free him from the emotional and relational mess he had created. The process was not easy, but John was able to make things right with God, cut off the affair with Sabrina, and receive his wife's forgiveness. As you can imagine, it took quite a while for John's marriage to stabilize, but over time God has brought healing and restoration to their relationship. John deeply regrets his sin and is diligent to walk more closely with God than ever before. "I know just how weak I am if I do not rely totally on the power of the Holy Spirit every day," he admits. "He gave me the power to stop the destructive, sinful pattern I had fallen into. I shudder to think where my marriage and family would be today had I not learned about the role of the Holy Spirit in my life."

"You Shall Receive Power..."

Frank, JoAnne, Stacy, Andrew and John have all discovered the secret that, tragically, has eluded most well-intentioned Christians around the world. Millions of believers do not know who the Holy Spirit is, let alone how to allow Him to release His power and peace in their lives. They coast through life in neutral gear, their spiritual joy dependent on the whims of circumstance, living a lukewarm Christianity, frustrated and disheartened by sin and compromise, never really experiencing the joy of moment-by-moment intimacy with our Lord.

Shortly before Jesus ascended to heaven, He promised His apostles, "You shall receive power when the Holy Spirit has come upon you" (Acts 1:8). Prior to Pentecost, these disciples were weak, defeated men. But on the glorious day when the power of heaven came upon them, they were empowered to "turn the world upside down" through their witness for Jesus Christ.

Through the centuries, the same Holy Spirit has given men and women His power to accomplish great things for the kingdom of God. He has filled Christians with love for the most trying of individuals; He has brought joy in the midst of heartache; He has generated peace in the most troubled soul; He has enabled fearful Christians to share His gospel boldly with others.

I know without a doubt that, had I not learned early in my Christian experience of my personal need for the Holy Spirit, I would have made a mess of my life. By nature I am rather shy and reserved. Talking with people about Jesus Christ doesn't always come easily for me. Yet, through four decades of ministry, the Holy Spirit has given me boldness to share Christ effectively, as well as an ability to train other Christians to do likewise.

In the course of leading a worldwide ministry, I have experienced His direction when it appeared that all options were closed. He has given me patience and peace when deadlines or financial obligations appeared impossible to meet. He has filled me with joy when my natural reaction would have been anger or despair.

I cannot accept accolades for the apparent success of my personal ministry or for the success of Campus Crusade for Christ, for I know that if I do not allow Him to direct me day by day, all my efforts for Christ will be fleshly and futile. But when I earnestly seek to yield to His guidance, I am confident that the very gates of hell cannot prevail against the ministry He wants to have in and through me.

Tap Into the Power Source

The power of the Holy Spirit is available to you — right now!

His power is helping Christians break stubborn habits.

He is changing stagnant, dwindling churches into dynamic, growing bodies of caring believers.

His power is helping men and women win over temptation, freeing them from bondage to sin and guilt.

His power is showing Christians how to truly love one another.

He is enabling believers to experience inner peace in the midst of trying circumstances.

He is helping thousands of Christians overcome the fear of sharing their faith in Christ with others.

If you would like to discover this power source, just take my hand. We are going on an exciting journey through some important scriptural concepts that somehow have gotten a little blurred over the centuries. They're going to sound amazingly simple. But when you apply them to your daily living, I guarantee that your life will never be the same.

The spiritual wildernesses of your life will diminish in size and frequency.

That perpetual roller coaster ride will stabilize.

You'll learn how to delight in the Lord every day — even when your situation doesn't seem so delightful.

You'll know what to do about the sins that have contributed to your constant defeats, and how to keep your conscience clean.

Boredom will become excitement. Hopelessness will become hope. Your walk with God will take on a new dimension of purpose and power because you are letting the Holy Spirit do His work in your life.

Are you ready for discovery? Let's take the first step.

*Understanding the inner conflict that
causes us so many problems*

2

Why Is It So Hard to Be Consistent?

*Without the presence of the quickening Spirit
there is no conviction, no regeneration, no sanctifica-
tion, no cleansing, no acceptable works. We can perform duties without Him, but our service is dull and
mechanical. Life is in the quickening Spirit.*
                                    W. A. Criswell

The attractive middle-aged couple inched their way forward through the small crowd that had gathered
around me. I had just spoken to a group of Christian executives and their spouses on the personal ministry of the Holy
Spirit, and the overall response had been enthusiastic. But
as this couple moved closer, I could see a troubled look in
their eyes.

"Can we talk with you alone?" the husband asked. "We
need your help on something."

After a few moments the three of us were able to move
to a secluded spot. There, Carl fidgeted a bit in his seat,

then began.

"I have a real problem with criticizing Jan," he said, nodding to his wife. "I just can't seem to help myself."

"In what ways do you criticize her?" I asked.

"He criticizes the way I look," Jan interjected.

"Yes," Carl admitted sheepishly. "I'm always on her case about dressing differently, or wearing her hair differently, or whatever."

Carl's admission took me by surprise, for I couldn't help noticing that Jan was a very attractive woman.

Her eyes moistened with tears. "It gets to me after a while. I try my best to please him, yet he finds fault with the way I cook, with my housekeeping, everything! If I try to defend myself, he'll accuse me of starting a fight." She paused a moment to dab at her eyes with a Kleenex. "I love him, but I don't know how much more of this I can take."

As the three of us talked further, it became clear that a critical spirit was one of Carl's ongoing problems. Instead of building up those he loved, he tore them down. He had tried many times to change, with only temporary success.

"I know God wants me to be more positive," he acknowledged. "I've prayed about it, and I've tried hard to do better, but I keep blowing it. Why is it so hard for me? How can I be more loving?"

Carl's problem is symptomatic of an inner battle we all face, the age-old conflict delineated by the apostle Paul in his letter to the Christians at Colossae:

> For he has rescued us out of the darkness and gloom
> of Satan's kingdom and brought us into the Kingdom of
> his dear Son, who bought our freedom with his blood and
> forgave us all our sins (Colossians 1:13,14).

There are two spiritual kingdoms, Paul taught, which we cannot see but which control the decisions and destiny of all men. Satan's kingdom, the one of darkness and gloom, promotes selfishness, pride, lust, arrogance, rebellion and despair. Man is born into Satan's kingdom and remains there either through ignorance, by choice or by default.

On the other hand, God's kingdom is one of light; it promotes eternal life, love for God and one another, selflessness, relational harmony and a joyful spirit. Membership in God's kingdom is attained only by deliberate choice, through receiving Jesus Christ as one's personal Savior and Lord.

The Freedom of Choice

When you became a Christian, you were liberated from Satan's kingdom and chose by faith to let Jesus Christ rule the throne of your heart. If you were sincere when you surrendered the control center of your heart to Him, He has promised never to leave nor forsake you (Hebrews 13:5).

However, God wants a family of thinking men and women, not puppets, so He continues to allow us the right of free choice. He wants us to *choose* whether we will obey Him. We can choose, every moment of every day, whether we want Christ to be in control or whether we want to retake the throne of our lives. When we yield to sin, we take back the control center—Christ is still in our lives, but He is no longer on the throne.

And Satan is well aware of this! Although we have been rescued from his seedy kingdom, he knows his kingdom can continue to influence us. His goal is to distract us from the purpose God has for us of becoming more and more like Jesus Christ. Paul described this ongoing conflict when he wrote to the Christians in Rome:

> I don't understand myself at all, for I really want to do what is right, but . . . I can't help myself, because

I'm no longer doing it. It is sin inside me that is stronger than I am that makes me do these evil things.

I know I am rotten through and through as far as my old sinful nature is concerned. No matter which way I turn I can't make myself do right. I want to but I can't (Romans 7:15-18).

Sound familiar? Carl didn't realize it at the time, but his words to me were almost identical to the apostle Paul's. And who among us hasn't at one time or another felt similar helplessness over our weakness in the face of temptation? The conflict between the kingdom of light and the kingdom of darkness is indeed real, and it is precisely the reason Christians find it difficult to be consistent in their walk with God. Satan has lost his quest for our souls, but he is a terribly sore loser. He will continue to tempt and distract in order to prevent us from realizing our full potential as children of the King.

As I shared these concepts with Carl and Jan, I took a sheet of paper and drew the following diagram:

OUR CONTROL CENTER

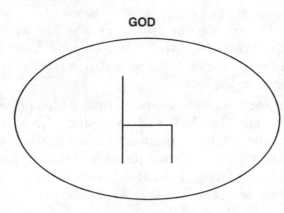

GOD

SATAN

"I recognize that from your talk this morning," Carl volunteered.

"Good. What does it represent?"

"Well, the circle represents my life, and the chair diagram represents a throne, the control center of my life."

"Right. What else?"

Jan chimed in, "There are two kingdoms seeking to influence us. One is God's kingdom, and other is Satan's kingdom. Before we became Christians, we were yielding to Satan's influence. But when we received Christ, we surrendered our 'control center' to Him."

"That's right," I commended them. Then I added to the diagram:

FREEDOM OF CHOICE

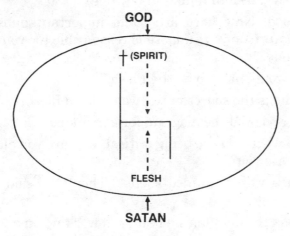

To explain the additions, I asked Carl and Jan to turn in their Bibles to Galatians 5:16,17. Here, the apostle Paul describes the ongoing conflict that takes place between the kingdom of God and the kingdom of Satan:

But I say, walk by the Spirit, and you will not carry out the desire of the Flesh.

For the Flesh sets its desire against the Spirit, and the Spirit against the Flesh; for these are in opposition to one another, so that you may not do the things that you please (NAS).

When we had finished reading these verses aloud, I pointed to the diagram and asked, "Carl, how many inner natures does the Bible say are battling for our attention?"

Carl studied the verses a moment. "Two. The Flesh and the Spirit."

"And when you became a Christian, you allowed Christ (Spirit) to reside on the throne of your life. But what can happen?"

Carl thought back to the lecture he had heard that morning. "God still gives us the freedom of choice, and we often allow Flesh to retake the throne."

"Good. Now here are some important questions: Which nature do you suppose is responsible for your critical attitude?"

"It would have to be the Flesh."

"Who is the source of the ways of the Flesh?"

He reviewed the diagram for a moment. "Satan."

"So when you are being critical, who are you allowing to influence you?"

There was a stunned silence. Then Carl said softly, "Satan."

I took the diagram we had been working on and completed it to illustrate what we had just discussed:

THE WRONG CHOICE

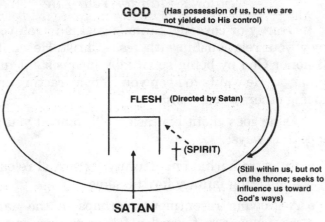

GOD (Has possession of us, but we are not yielded to His control)

FLESH (Directed by Satan)

✝ (SPIRIT)

(Still within us, but not on the throne; seeks to influence us toward God's ways)

SATAN

(Seeks control of us through the Flesh)

"When we are Christians who live in sin, we are still in God's possession, but we have yielded to the influence of Satan and given Flesh control of the throne," I explained. "Christ is no longer on the throne, but He continues to seek to influence us and bring us back to God's ways. As long as we allow our fleshly nature to remain on the throne, though, our attitudes and actions will be selfish and sinful."

As we talked, the seriousness of the conflict became clearer to both Carl and Jan. Christ wants to be on the throne, but He will remain there only as long as He is a welcome resident. Meanwhile, the enemy does everything in his power to destroy our intimacy with the Savior, to ruin our relationships with others, and to discredit our witness to the world.

This diagram helped Carl and Jan picture the ongoing battle that rages within us between the Flesh and the Spirit. As we'll see in a later chapter, Carl was able to build upon this concept to help conquer his critical attitude.

Satan's Plan for Your Life

Overtly or covertly, Satan's goal is to rob you of the joy of your relationship with Jesus Christ. He wants you to dishonor God by being spiritually inconsistent, unhappy, lethargic. He wants to keep you from attracting and introducing others to our Lord.

As he goes about his task, he'll come at you in many appealing ways:

- An extramarital opportunity for sexual release, or a lingering fantasy for the same
- A growing resentment, perhaps in the name of righteousness, toward a fellow worker or church member
- An opportunity to display your wit through negativism or cynicism
- A chance to take supplies home from the office ("after all I've done for them, I've certainly earned a few privileges . . .")
- A twinge of jealousy when a neighbor, friend or relative achieves a higher financial level than you
- An opportunity to watch a pornographic video ("just so I can pray more specifically about the problem")
- A choice between some additional sleep and that Quiet Time in the Word
- A perfect opening to "put down" your spouse or other loved one
- A chance to spread some juicy gossip or sow discord
- An easy way out of an obvious witnessing opportunity
- Getting so busy doing the *work* of the Lord that you

ignore your *walk* with the Lord

Over the years, Satan has come at me with many of these temptations. I'm sure that in years to come he will dangle many more before me. It is humbling and sobering to know that, even after almost fifty years as a Christian, I am susceptible to any one of the enemy's tactics if I do not rely totally on God's loving power moment by moment. The conflict between the two kingdoms is a strong one and the attraction to Satan's kingdom is real.

The Life-Giving Spirit

But I can testify wholeheartedly that, while God in His sovereign way allows the conflict between good and evil to go on, He has provided each of us with the ultimate weapon against Satan. The apostle Paul describes it this way:

> Who will free me from my slavery to this deadly lower nature? Thank God! It has been done by Jesus Christ our Lord. He has set me free.
>
> So there is now no condemnation awaiting those who belong to Christ Jesus. For *the power of the life-giving Spirit—and His power is mine through Jesus Christ—has freed me from the vicious circle of sin and death.*
>
> So now we can obey God's laws if we follow after the Holy Spirit and no longer obey the old evil nature within us (Romans 7:25 – 8:4).

The "life-giving Spirit." The Holy Spirit of God the Father and God the Son. Jesus said that when He left earth He would send the Spirit to do His work in us and through us. He promised that we would receive power from the Spirit to do great things in His name, to resist the pull of the kingdom of darkness, to live a life that brings honor to Him and joy and fulfillment to us.

Jesus keeps His promises! That same Holy Spirit who

empowered the apostle Paul centuries ago is available to you and me today. Paul wrote from personal experience, "Walk by the Spirit, and you will not carry out the desire of the flesh" (Galatians 5:16, NAS). Do you want purpose and power? Walk by the Spirit. Do you want to conquer a bad habit? Walk by the Spirit. Want to introduce a friend to Christ? Walk by the Spirit.

What does it mean to "walk by the Spirit"? That's what you're going to discover in our journey through these pages. The next stop is an important one: a look at who the Holy Spirit is and what He wants to do in your life.

FOR REFLECTION, DISCUSSION AND ACTION

1. Do you agree with the statement of W. A. Criswell at the beginning of this chapter? Why or why not?

2. In what ways have you sensed the conflict between the Flesh and the Spirit in your life?

3. Although Christians have been rescued from the kingdom of Satan, why do you suppose God has allowed Satan to continue trying to influence us?

4. Give a general description of the types of "messages" that come to you from the Flesh. What are some common denominators that will help you recognize that these messages are from Satan?

5. Give a general description of the types of "messages" that come to you from the Spirit. What are some common denominators that will help you recognize that these messages are from God?

6. What does Galatians 5:16 mean to you personally? During the next week, memorize and reflect on the command and the promise of this verse: "Walk by the Spirit, and you will not carry out the desire of the flesh."

3

Comforter, Helper, Teacher, Guide

*He who does not know God the Holy Spirit does
not know God at all.*

Thomas Arnold

Sally was almost penniless. When her husband Jeb died years before, his life insurance had paid off the mortgage, but that was about it.

Now the house was deteriorating around her. The car had been junked long ago when she couldn't keep up with the repair and insurance bills. She got by on just a few dollars each week for groceries, and when the electric bill got too high she decided to live by Coleman stove and candlelight.

So Sally rarely left home. How could she when everything cost money? Coffee at the cafe was eighty-five cents. Even with her senior citizen's discount, movies cost $3. A walk to the park required shoes, and Sally's only remaining pair were clinging together by a few bits of thread.

So day after day, Sally stayed at home and creaked back and forth in her rocking chair. *Life was supposed to be better than this,* she thought. *It started out so great. So full of promise. But now it's passed me by.*

And so she lived—just barely lived—for years. Destitute. Lonely. Defeated. Until one day, when an old acquaintance from across the country remembered her childhood friend and decided to look her up.

Miriam was heartbroken when she saw Sally's living conditions. She decided to stay a few days to try to encourage her friend and help straighten up the house.

And in the course of helping her old friend, Miriam made a startling discovery.

Tucked away in the file drawer of Jeb's old roll-top desk was a folder labeled *"FOR SALLY."* Inside, Miriam found an old bank savings book. The last entry had been made twenty-two years earlier, just before Jeb had died. The bank book indicated a balance of $87,000.

But that wasn't all. The folder also contained a yellowed envelope, sealed and inscribed with Jeb's handwriting:

To Sally, With Love Forever

"Do you know what this is?" Miriam asked.

Sally searched her memory. She remembered the last days of her beloved husband, the tender words that had passed between them as they realized that the end was near.

Then the memory hit her. In the grief and heartache of the days and months following Jeb's death, she had forgotten one of the things he had said: "When I'm gone . . . a file for you . . . in my desk. Important."

Now, as Miriam watched, Sally opened the envelope carefully. Inside was a single folded page and a key. Sally began to read:

> *My Dearest Love—*
>
> *My time with you draws short, but I want you to know that I have provided everything you will need once I am gone. Check the bank book in this file. Then take this key to the bank with you. In loving remembrance of me, please enjoy life to the full!*
>
> *With love forever,*
>
> *Jeb*

Sally and Miriam discovered that the key was to a safety deposit box at the bank. As they lifted the metal lid, their eyes widened as they discovered several bundles of cash totaling $32,000, a pile of stock certificates, and three folders of rare coins.

That afternoon a stock broker informed them that the stock certificates were worth $550,000 on the current market. A rare coin dealer appraised the coin collection at $47,000. The bank calculated twenty-two years' interest on the savings account, which brought its total from $87,000 to more than $254,000. All told, Sally was worth more than $883,000! She had been living in misery and despair when more money than she would ever need had been available to her all along.

Spiritual Poverty

When a friend first told me Sally's story, I was moved with emotion—for Sally is a vivid illustration of the bittersweet way in which many Christians also live. Although God has promised us all the strength and help we will ever need, many of us try to "go it alone" because we are unaware of the boundless resources God has provided in the person of the Holy Spirit. As a result, we live like Sally—unfulfilled, fruitless and spiritually malnourished—while the key to joy and abundance is within our grasp.

In the course of our ministry, we have surveyed many thousands of Christians in churches around the world. Sadly, nearly 95 percent of the respondents have indicated that they have little knowledge of who the Holy Spirit is or why He exists. It is interesting to note that among these same believers, an overwhelming majority have indicated that they feel deeply discouraged about their spiritual growth and their levels of commitment and consistency.

Another friend recently told me how shocked he was as he participated in a Sunday school class in which Christian adults, several of whom had been believers for decades, were sharing their thoughts about the Holy Spirit.

"I think He is the warm feeling we have when we think about God," said one.

"Maybe He is the good memories of Jesus Christ, just like the 'spirit' of '76," another speculated.

A gum-popping young woman chimed in, "I kinda look on Him like, you know, The Force—from *Star Wars*?"

Many in this class knew that the Holy Spirit is the third Person of the Trinity, but they couldn't go any further than that. My friend told me he got the distinct impression that most of these Christian men and women acknowledged the Holy Spirit as "a member of the family, but more as a distant cousin whom no one understands. As a result, He is not invited to family gatherings."

How tragic and true is A. W. Tozer's observation: "The idea of the Spirit held by the average church member is so vague as to be nearly nonexistent." I am personally convinced that if today's Christians better understood the Bible's basic teaching about the Holy Spirit and then invited Him to release His power in their lives each day, they would experience unprecedented joy and personal fulfillment. More than that, our verbal and nonverbal witness for Jesus Christ would sweep the world!

Who Is the Holy Spirit?

While there is a degree of divine mystery to the nature of the Holy Spirit, He definitely is not a bundle of warm feelings or good memories, or some vague cosmic force. From Genesis to Revelation, God's Word teaches that the Holy Spirit is a person, and He is God. In the next few pages, we will examine some of the scriptural evidence. Please do not skip over these verses lightly, for they are important statements regarding the nature and ministry of the Holy Spirit in your life!

The Holy Spirit Is a Person

The Bible tells us that the Holy Spirit possesses intellect (1 Corinthians 2:11), will (1 Corinthians 12:11) and emotion (Romans 15:30). In addition, He performs specific actions which cannot be performed by some impersonal ethereal force:

He speaks: "And while they were ministering to the Lord and fasting, the Holy Spirit said, 'Set apart for Me Barnabas and Saul for the work to which I have called them' " (Acts 13:2, NAS).

He teaches: "But the Helper, the Holy Spirit, whom the Father will send in My name, He will teach you all things, and bring to your remembrance all that I said to you" (John 14:26, NAS).

He guides: "But when He, the Spirit of truth, comes, He will guide you into all truth" (John 16:13, NAS).

He convicts: "But I tell you the truth, it is to your advantage that I go away; for if I do not go away, the Helper shall not come to you; but if I go, I will send Him to you. And He, when He comes, will convict the world concerning sin, and righteousness, and judgment" (John 16:7,8, NAS).

He commands: "And the Spirit said to Philip, 'Go up and join this chariot' " (Acts 8:29, NAS).

He helps: "And in the same way the Spirit also helps our weakness" (Romans 8:26, NAS).

He comforts: "I will pray the Father, and he shall give you another Comforter, that he may abide with you forever" (John 14:16, KJV).

The Greek word used in John 14:26 and 15:26 for the Holy Spirit is *paraclete,* meaning the "one called along beside" the Christian. It connotes companionship, comfort, help; it also carries the meaning of one who energizes, strengthens and empowers the believer.

Such actions as these are not possible for a concept or "force" to perform. These acts are things only a person can do. In his perceptive book *Secret Power,* Dwight L. Moody writes of the importance of acknowledging the personality of the Holy Spirit:

> I was a Christian a long time before I found out that the Holy [Spirit] was a person. Now this is something a great many don't seem to understand, but if you will just take up the Bible and see what Christ has to say about the Holy Spirit, you will find that He always spoke of Him as a person . . . Observe the pronouns *He* and *Him.* I want to call attention to this fact that whenever Christ spoke of the Holy [Spirit] He spoke of Him as a person, not a mere influence, and if we want to honor the Holy [Spirit] let us bear in mind that He is one of the Trinity, a personality of the Godhead.[1]

The Holy Spirit Is God

The Holy Spirit is not only a person, but He also is a divine person. He possesses characteristics and performs works that can only be attributed to Almighty God Himself. This is what enables Him to do the powerful works in us that Jesus promised He would do!

He is eternal: "How much more will the blood of Christ, who through the eternal Spirit offered Himself without blemish to God, cleanse your conscience from dead works to serve the living God?" (Hebrews 9:14, NAS).

He is omnipresent (present everywhere): "Where can I go from Thy Spirit? Or where can I flee from Thy presence?" (Psalm 139:7, NAS).

He is omniscient (all-knowing): "For to us God revealed them through the Spirit; for the Spirit searches all things, even the depths of God. For who among men knows the thoughts of a man except the spirit of the man, which is in him? Even so the thoughts of God no one knows except the Spirit of God" (1 Corinthians 2:10,11, NAS).

He is omnipotent (all-powerful): "The Spirit of God has made me, and the breath of the Almighty gives me life" (Job 33:4, NAS).

He inspired the Scriptures: "For no prophecy was ever made by an act of human will, but men moved by the Holy Spirit spoke from God" (2 Peter 1:21, NAS).

He caused the miraculous conception of Christ: "And the angel answered and said to her, 'The Holy Spirit will come upon you, and the power of the Most High will over-shadow you; and for that reason the holy offspring shall be called the Son of God' " (Luke 1:35, NAS).

He gives believers new, holy natures: "God chose from the very first to give you salvation, cleansing you by the work of the Holy Spirit . . ." (2 Thessalonians 2:13).

He produces the fruit of the Spirit: "And the fruit of the Spirit is love, joy, peace, patience, kindness, goodness, faithfulness, gentleness and self-control" (Galatians 5:22,23, NAS).

He empowers for witnessing: "But you shall receive power when the Holy Spirit has come upon you; and you shall be My witnesses . . ." (Acts 1:8, NAS).

These divine attributes and powerful works could

never be performed by a mere influence or impersonal force, nor by an ordinary person. Only God Himself has the power to be and do all of these wonderful things among His people. The Holy Spirit is Almighty God!

The Divine Mystery

"Okay, all these Scripture verses help, but I'm still confused," a young man once said to me. "I keep hearing about the Holy Trinity—God in three persons, Father, Son and Holy Spirit. Are they one and the same, or aren't they? And why don't we just leave this confusing stuff alone and concentrate on Jesus?"

Here, any theologian must admit, is where the finiteness of human thought becomes inadequate to comprehend the infinite ways of God. Our limited minds simply do not think in terms of the Holy Trinity, in which God the Father, God the Son and God the Holy Spirit are coequal members of the Godhead. Our brains do not fathom how there can be only one God manifesting Himself in three persons. One day we will enjoy His holy presence and all will be made clear to us; in this life, however, the Trinity remains a divine mystery.

Our best efforts to explain the Trinity fall far short of its reality. I might say that as a man I am also a husband, a father, and the president of a worldwide ministry. One man, three functions. Or I could say that H_2O is three different things: it can be water, ice or steam. One formula, three forms. But the Trinity is far deeper, wider, and greater than these awkward illustrations.

What we do know from God's Word is that we have one God who manifests Himself in three distinct persons. Charles Ryrie, in *The Ryrie Study Bible*, notes that when Jesus said "I and the Father are one" (John 10:30, NAS), He used the neuter form of *one*, which "rules out the meaning that [the Father and Son] are one person." Rather, the meaning is that "The Father and Son [and, it follows, the Holy Spirit] are in perfect unity in their natures and actions."[2] All three have the mind and attributes of God, so there is never conflict or disagreement among the three. The three are one; the one is three. Later in the same conversation, Jesus said, "The Father is in Me, and I in the Father" (John 10:38). Indeed, a divine mystery.

As incomprehensible as it is, the Holy Trinity is real and requires our belief and honor. One of my seminary professors once said, "To try to understand the Trinity is to lose one's mind; to deny the Trinity is to lose one's soul." Most of us do not comprehend gravity, yet we accept its reality. Vance Havner once said, "I don't understand all about electricity, but I'm not going to sit around in the dark till I do."

In like manner, the Trinity will never be comprehended in human terms, but that should not preclude our wholehearted reliance on its existence. It becomes one of those areas of Christianity in which faith is faith, based on the unshakable word of our Lord Jesus Christ Himself that the Holy Spirit is real and has been at work in the lives of men and women through the ages.

Why should we be aware of the Holy Spirit's role in our lives? Because He is our personal manifestation of the living God and of the living Christ. He is the power of Almighty God at our disposal to honor His ways and do His work; He is Jesus Christ residing within us to keep His promise "that they might have life, and might have it abundantly" (John 10:10, NAS).

What He Wants to Do for You

The Holy Spirit is vitally interested in you! His mission is to give you the strength and guidance you need to accomplish God's purpose for you on this earth.

What is our purpose? I like the way the Westminster Shorter Catechism phrases it: "The purpose of man is to glorify God and to enjoy Him forever." That's why we are here—to bring honor, praise and glory to our Lord and Savior, and to enjoy the riches of His presence in our lives. That's joy! That's consistency! And God has provided the Holy Spirit to make it possible.

Earlier in this chapter we listed several key Scriptures that emphasize both the person and the deity of the Holy Spirit. Please take just a moment to page back and read through them again. As you review these rich passages, you will observe at least four important roles the Holy Spirit wants to fulfill in your life.

Your Personal Comforter

Have you ever been around a fellow believer who, even though struck by tragedy and heartache, seemed to radiate a supernatural peace in the midst of his tears? Your first reaction may have been, *He can't be for real!*

But the peace you observed is most likely the inner working of the Holy Spirit in that person's life. God's Spirit doesn't shelter us from human hurts (Jesus Himself experienced the full gamut of physical and emotional pain, even torturous death on the cross for our sins). But in the midst of our hurts, God's Spirit can give us the peace that passes all understanding—an inner assurance that God is indeed in control and that we can trust Him to work "all things together for good" (Romans 8:28).

When Jesus said, "I will pray the Father, and he shall give you another Comforter, that he may abide with you for ever" (John 14:16, KJV), He was talking to you and me! The Holy Spirit is our personal Comforter who can give us supernatural strength, courage and peace when all around might seem to be crumbling.

Your Personal Helper

What is your Achilles' heel? Anger? Lust? Self-importance? A critical spirit? God is fully aware of the spiritual
battle that rages between the kingdoms of light and darkness, and He has sent the Holy Spirit to give us power to
overcome temptation. Since His purpose is to glorify God,
He is constantly available to help *us* glorify God!

Your Personal Teacher

As you read and study the Scriptures, the Holy Spirit
will instruct you in righteousness and help you unearth dis-
coveries that you can apply to your walk with God. As you
listen earnestly to a sermon or lecture, He will point out to
you the ways in which God wants you to think, speak and
act. When a fresh insight hits you that reveals more of the
majesty of God, this is the Holy Spirit at work in you.

Moreover, like the best teachers, He frequently ap-
plies those truths with us in real-life situations. When a
problem arises, He will remind us of an appropriate Scripture verse we once studied or memorized. Or if we suddenly begin doubting God's provision, He will whisper, *Fear
not. Remember how God provided for you yesterday?*

Think of it: The Holy Spirit has a vested interest in
teaching you the ways of God! What a privilege it is for us
to have personal access to His divine, omniscient wisdom.

Your Personal Guide

The Christian who wants to live for God will often
sense that there is a sort of inner barometer inside him —
a measure of deep peace when he is in God's will and a dis-
turbing lack of peace when he has ventured outside God's
will. This again is the Holy Spirit at work.

As your personal guide, the Holy Spirit will convict
you of unconfessed sin by causing that inner barometer to
plunge. He will seek to prevent you from sinning in the first

place by bringing a scriptural command to mind, or by giving you a sense of unrest and impurity about the step you are contemplating. He will steer you toward God's will as you seek His wisdom in the decisions you must make.

His Resources Are at Our Disposal

Comforter, Helper, Teacher, Guide. The Holy Spirit's purpose is to glorify Christ, and He does so by empowering and enabling you and me to glorify God by the way we live. His resources are at our disposal. If we do not appropriate them, we can only live like poor Sally, struggling through a meager existence when vast riches are at our command.

But when we give the Holy Spirit control of our lives, the spiritual bank vault opens wide. The Lord God Almighty gives us everything we need to honor Him and experience life to the full, for "out of his glorious, unlimited resources he will give you the mighty inner strengthening of his Holy Spirit" (Ephesians 3:16).

The next stop on our journey will show how we can make that happen.

FOR REFLECTION, DISCUSSION AND ACTION

1. How would you describe your present spiritual journey: ☐ Exciting, fulfilling, one that glorifies God;   ☐ Dull, unfulfilling, one that probably doesn't glorify God;   ☐ Somewhere in between. Explain your answer, and give some specific reasons.

2. Before you studied this chapter, how would you have answered the question, "Who is the Holy Spirit and what does He mean to me?"

3. Imagine that a relatively new Christian has asked you the same question: "Who is the Holy Spirit and what does He mean to me?" How would you answer him now?

4. Reflect upon and discuss the meaning of the Westminster Shorter Catechism statement: "The purpose of man is to glorify God and to enjoy Him forever." In what ways does God want us to glorify Him? In what ways are we to enjoy Him?

5. What is the Holy Spirit's purpose? In what ways does He go about fulfilling His purpose in the Christian's life?

6. Have you recently sensed the comfort, help, teaching and guidance of the Holy Spirit? If so, give an example. If you have not experienced His closeness, why do you think you haven't?

7. Memorize and reflect upon the personal significance of the apostle Paul's promise in Ephesians 3:16: "Out of his glorious, unlimited resources he will give you the mighty inner strengthening of his Holy Spirit."

---

1. Dwight L. Moody, *Secret Power* (Ventura, CA: Regal Books, 1987), pp. 29-30.
2. Charles C. Ryrie, *The Ryrie Study Bible (NAS)* (Chicago: Moody Press, 1978), footnote to John 10:30.

Spirit-filled living is not optional for the Christian. It is a command of God.

4

What Does It Mean to Be "Filled" With the Spirit?

The Spirit-filled life is no mystery revealed to a select few, no goal difficult of attainment. To trust and to obey is the substance of the whole matter.
V. Raymond Edman

Contrary to popular thought, the Ten Commandments were not the Ten Suggestions. When God gives a command to His people, He means it. Imagine Him sitting beside you as you review His commandments. "Well, Lord," you say, "this command sounds all right, so I'll follow it, okay? But this next one seems like it would be awfully inconvenient. I'll pass on it, if You don't mind. Number three sounds do-able. Number four, maybe—if I can fit it into my schedule. But your next command? You must not have understood my situation when You wrote *this* one!"

Since there is nothing in the Scriptures to indicate

that God grades on the curve, it is reasonable to assume that He would be highly displeased with such an attitude. In fact, Jesus taught that God measures our love for Him by the extent and genuineness of our obedience: "If you love Me, you will keep My commandments" (John 14:15; also see 16-24).

Fortunately, few dedicated Christians would intentionally assume such a cavalier attitude toward God. Yet there is one very important command from Him that many Christians regularly disobey — a command which is vital to our personal joy and effectiveness.

That command is found in the apostle Paul's letter to the Christians at Ephesus. In the midst of a discourse on the practices of Christian living, Paul writes: "And do not get drunk with wine, for that is dissipation, but *be filled with the Spirit*" (Ephesians 5:18, NAS).

Notice that Paul did not write, "Now folks, you may want to consider being filled with the Spirit." Rather, he was specific and firm. "Do not get drunk with wine." (Don't let things of this world control you, your thoughts or your priorities.) "Be filled with the Spirit." (Instead, let the Holy Spirit of God, with all His divine attributes, control and empower you.)

Since all Scripture is inspired by God (2 Timothy 3:16), we know that Paul's command is God's command. He specifically requires each Christian to be filled with His Holy Spirit.

What Being "Filled" Means

When you invited Jesus Christ into your life, the Holy Spirit did several important things.

First, He came to "dwell" within you, as Jesus promised when He said, "if anyone hears My voice and opens the door, I will come in to Him, and will dine with him, and he with Me" (Revelation 3:20, NAS). Paul wrote of "the Holy Spirit who is in you, whom you have from God" (1 Corinthians 6:19, NAS). If you were sincere in your commitment to Christ, He "will never leave you nor forsake you" (Hebrews 13:5, NAS).

Second, the Holy Spirit gave you "new birth." "Unless one is born again," Jesus told Nicodemus, "he cannot see the kingdom of God . . . unless one is born of water *and the Spirit,* he cannot enter into the kingdom of God" (John 3:3-6, NAS). When you received Christ as your Savior and Lord, the Holy Spirit rescued you from Satan's kingdom and delivered you into God's kingdom. You became a child of God, a member of His eternal family. That means you can enjoy the fullness of His nature and provision, and that when your time on this earth is finished you will go to heaven to bask in God's presence forever.

Third, the Holy Spirit placed His "seal" on you. "Having also believed, you were sealed in Him with the Holy Spirit of promise . . . sealed for the day of redemption" (Ephesians 1:13; 4:30, NAS).

In Paul's time, and through the centuries since, a wax seal was often placed on an envelope or other important document to (1) announce to the receiver the authority and importance of the sender, and (2) to assure the receiver that no one had opened the document or tampered with its contents. Paul used this word picture of an "official seal" to help Christians envision how God's Holy Spirit protects us. He places His "seal" on us to indicate that we are children of God and belong to Him, and that He will keep us secure from Satan and the wages of sin.

Fourth, the Holy Spirit "baptized" you into the Body of Christ. The physical act of baptism symbolizes the individual's public relinquishment or burial of the old life and the appropriation of his new life in Christ. In His Great Commission, Jesus instructed, "Go therefore and make disciples of all the nations, baptizing them in the name of the Father and the Son and the Holy Spirit" (Matthew 28:19, NAS). This physical act of baptism is a public acknowledgment of what the Holy Spirit did inside you when you received Christ—He buried your old life by God's grace and forgiveness, and gave you new life in the family of God. "For by one Spirit we are all baptized into one body," Paul wrote in 1 Corinthians 12:13.

Elsewhere Paul likened this process to the discarding of dirty old clothes for a new wardrobe: "For all of you who were baptized into Christ have clothed yourselves in Christ" (Galatians 3:27, NAS). His analogy gives us a fascinating word picture of how we virtually become a "suit of clothes" for Christ, allowing Him to walk, think, talk and act from inside us. We are the outer garment; He is the inner source.

One "Indwelling," Many "Fillings"

So we can see that if you have received Jesus Christ as your Savior and Lord, you do not need to invite the Holy Spirit to come into your life. He already lives within you, for He came to dwell within you the moment you trusted Christ as your Savior and Lord. There is but one indwelling by the Holy Spirit, one rebirth by the Holy Spirit, and one baptism by the Holy Spirit, for all of these glorious acts take place the moment a person receives Christ.

However, there can be many *fillings* by the Holy Spirit. In the Greek language, in which the New Testament was originally written, the meaning of "be filled with the Spirit" is clearer than in most English translations. "Be filled" literally means to *be constantly and continually filled, controlled and empowered with the Holy Spirit every moment of every day*. In other words, we are to consciously give Jesus Christ the control of our lives every moment, looking to His Spirit for guidance and strength and yielding to His leading and conviction.

Because He promised never to leave or forsake us, He will not exit our lives when we sin; but neither will He forcibly maintain control of our wills when we contemplate sin. God created us with freedom of choice, and we can choose whether we will obey or disobey Him. He wants us to obey Him by choice, not by coercion. Thus, if we choose to yield to Him, He will lead us. If we choose to sin, He will let us.

The Key: Keeping Christ on the Throne

To better understand this concept of being "filled" with the Spirit, let's return to the illustration of the throne. The throne represents your "control center," or your will. When you received Christ as Savior and Lord, you invited Him into your life and onto the throne—you deliberately surrendered the control and guidance of your life to Him.

Before you became a Christian, you were what the Bible calls a "natural" person:

NATURAL MAN

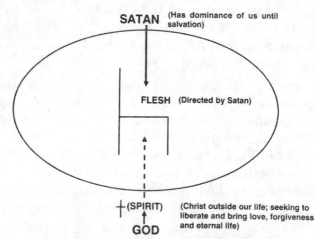

SATAN (Has dominance of us until salvation)

FLESH (Directed by Satan)

+(SPIRIT) (Christ outside our life; seeking to liberate and bring love, forgiveness and eternal life)

GOD

The circle represents your life, and the throne represents your control center or will. You were living under Satan's dominance and your fleshly nature, directed by Satan, was "on the throne," controlling your life. Christ was outside of your life, knocking at the door, wanting to liberate you from Satan's dominance by bringing you His love, forgiveness and eternal life.

"But a natural man does not accept the things of the Spirit of God; for they are foolishness to him; and he cannot understand them, because they are spiritually appraised" (1 Corinthians 2:14, NAS).

Then you surrendered your life to Jesus Christ:

SPIRITUAL MAN

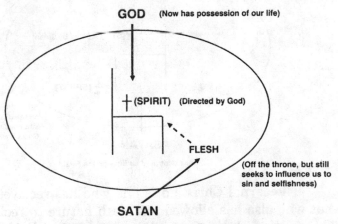

GOD   (Now has possession of our life)

+ (SPIRIT)   (Directed by God)

FLESH

(Off the throne, but still seeks to influence us to sin and selfishness)

SATAN

(Seeks to control us through the Flesh)

At your invitation, Christ entered your life and took the throne to guide you and strengthen you to live for Him. At this moment, His Holy Spirit indwelled you, gave you new birth, sealed you for heaven, and baptized you into the body of believers. With Christ (Spirit) on the throne, you were "filled" (directed and empowered) by the Holy Spirit.

"But he who is spiritual appraises all things" (1 Corinthians 2:15, NAS).

The act of staying "filled" with the Spirit is the act of deliberately keeping Christ on the throne of your life. He will not demand control against your will. If, despite His guidance and warning, you wish to yield to the influence of the Flesh and wrest control away from Him for a period of overt or covert sin, He will sorrowfully step down. When you are in this state of unconfessed sin, God's Word describes you as one who is "carnal":

CARNAL MAN

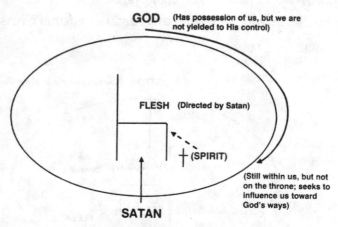

The carnal Christian is one who has received Christ but who also has allowed his Flesh nature to reclaim the throne through sin. God still has possession of this person, and Christ is still in his life, but the individual is not yielded to God. Rather, Satan has succeeded in influencing and controlling this Christian through the Flesh.

"And I, brethren, could not speak to you as to spiritual men, but as to carnal men, as to babes in Christ. I gave you milk to drink, not solid food; for you were not yet able to receive it. Indeed, even now you are not yet able, for you are still carnal. For since there is jealousy and strife among you, are you not fleshly, and are you not walking like mere men?" (1 Corinthians 3:1-3).

The state of carnality, or unconfessed sin, is a miserable existence. It is like poor Sally, who was surrounded by riches designated for her enjoyment but who failed to open the file folder which held the key to the bank vault. The carnal Christian has cut off fellowship with God and impeded His flow of blessing.

Yet, sadly, this is where millions of Christians rest today—back on the throne of their lives. By remaining on the throne, we in effect are saying that we do not fully trust God, that we think *our* way of doing things is better. Our lives may be characterized by some or all of the following traits:

- unbelief
- lack of faith
- disobedience
- loss of love for God and for others
- poor prayer life
- little desire for Bible study
- a legalistic attitude
- impure thoughts
- jealousy
- guilt
- anxiety
- discouragement
- a negative or critical spirit
- frustration
- lethargy
- aimlessness

- materialism
- self-centeredness
- self-importance

Are these the qualities of a winner? Does the carnal Christian appear to be someone who is going to attract others to the Savior and help win his world for Jesus Christ? Perhaps this explains why in too many cases the impact of Christians on their communities has been negligible or even negative.

"Part-time Christian"

Dwayne recalls how this carnal state had robbed him of his Christian joy. "I had been a Christian since I was a child, and grew up attending church two or three times a week," Dwayne remembers. "From all those Sunday school classes and sermons I knew the Bible pretty well. As I grew older, if anyone had asked me, I would have proclaimed that I loved the Lord and that He was the most important person in my life. But in reality, that wasn't true.

"Over the years, in very subtle ways, other people and things had become more important to me than my relationship with Jesus Christ. Oh, Christianity was always a part of me, but not *all* of me. I gradually put school, women, career, money, and other activities higher on my priority list. Those are the things I thought about and devoted my time to."

In his adulthood, Dwayne had a restless gnawing in the back of his conscience. "I knew I wasn't truly fulfilled . . . I was happy on the surface but I had little joy coming from within. I took my family to church and led them in prayers and tried to center my home around God, but I felt like I was going through the motions."

One day, Dwayne's friend Rob took him to lunch. Rob

had attended a training conference at his church and was excited about a concept he had learned. "Rob took a napkin and drew the three diagrams representing the natural, spiritual and carnal person," Dwayne recalls. "When he described the symptoms of carnality, I realized he was describing *me* — perfectly!"

With Rob's friendly help, Dwayne learned the steps he needed to take to break free of his restless, carnal condition. On his way home from the office that night, Dwayne pulled into the parking lot of a city park and prayed, asking God's forgiveness and inviting Him to return to the throne of his life.

Dwayne reports, "I still fall into some of my old habits and sinful patterns, but I don't stay there for long. I know now that I don't have to let Satan defeat me. The key is to keep Christ on the throne — to be continually directed and empowered by the Holy Spirit. I don't have to be a part-time, uncommitted Christian. I only regret that I wasted so much time before making this discovery!"

Where Do You Stand?

Does the above list of symptoms describe *your* spiritual life? If you recognize some of those traits as being yours, it is possible that you have moved out of fellowship with God through unconfessed sin and have retaken the throne of your life.

But the good news is that you don't have to continue to live this way! Our Lord stands ready and willing to resume His rightful position of authority on the throne if you will let Him.

In the next chapter we'll see how.

FOR REFLECTION, DISCUSSION AND ACTION

1. Do you tend to be selective as to which of God's commands you will try to obey? Give an example or two.

2. Why is it so important for Christians to obey the command to be filled with the Spirit?

3. Review what the Holy Spirit did for you when you received Christ. Describe in your own words why the "indwelling," "new birth," "seal" and "baptism" by the Holy Spirit are significant to you.

4. Memorize the definition of "be filled": *to be constantly and continually filled, controlled and empowered with the Holy Spirit every moment of every day.* What does this definition mean to you?

5. Why is it that, while there is one "indwelling," one "new birth," one "sealing" and one "baptism" by the Holy Spirit, there can be many "fillings"?

6. Of the three types of people (natural, spiritual, carnal), which do you think best describes your present spiritual journey? Why?

It is impossible for both Jesus Christ and the human ego to reside on the throne at the same time.

5

How to Be Filled With the Holy Spirit

Every time we say, "I believe in the Holy Spirit," we mean that we believe that there is a living God able and willing to enter human personality and change it.

J. B. Phillips

In the last chapter we saw that God has given every Christian a clear command to be directed and empowered by the Holy Spirit. If His Spirit is not in control of our lives, we are in a sinful, carnal state that is both displeasing to Him and miserable to us.

Ned, by his own admission, had lived as a carnal Christian for several months. God seemed far away from him. "I had become spiritually lazy," he admits. "I had little desire for fellowship with the Lord or with other Christians. I rarely spent time in the Word. I found my mind dwelling on lustful, impure thoughts. I put up a good front, but deep inside I was a spiritual wasteland."

Then came a weekend revival emphasis at his church. The evangelist asked a question that Ned had seen on a poster somewhere:

If you feel far from God, guess who moved?

"That question nailed me," Ned recalls. "I felt far from God, and I realized that my spiritual dryness was my fault."

As the evangelist challenged people to walk to the front of the church and rededicate themselves, Ned became convicted of his need to restore his relationship with Jesus Christ.

"But I didn't know what to do, and no one could show me. I walked forward during the invitation, and I knelt at the altar with the others and prayed and cried and waited. Some other men came and prayed with me. I guess I expected some kind of big emotional breakthrough or bolt of lightning from the Lord, but it never came.

"The next night I did the same thing. As the evangelist spoke, I felt guilty all over again. I got on my knees and waited for something to happen, something from heaven to zap me and tell me everything was okay."

When the weekend ended, Ned felt some sense of relief, but he was still discouraged and empty, as though he had missed out on some special magic or chorus of angels singing from the heavens.

"Several months later I attended a Lay Institute for Evangelism sponsored by several of the churches in our town. There, I learned about the personal ministry of the Holy Spirit and how to make things right with God.

"I learned that I had been seeking an emotional experience, when being filled with the Holy Spirit is really a deliberate, rational act of surrender on our part. Being filled is simply the act of keeping Christ on the throne of my life in obedience to His command in Ephesians 5:18.

"I thank God that I learned this important principle. It has changed my life!"

Like Ned, many wayward Christians seek some kind of vague emotional experience when rededicating themselves to Jesus Christ. What they do not realize is that He stands ready and willing to restore His fullness to us through His Holy Spirit, if we will only let Him. We don't have to pray, fast and wait for some mystical or emotional breakthrough. We don't have to beg and plead with God to be filled with the Spirit. According to God's Word, we are filled, simply and miraculously, by faith and faith alone in response to His commands and promises.

We Are Filled by Faith

How did you become a Christian? Not by reciting a prayer, nor by an emotional experience. You became a Christian *by faith*, by putting your trust in Jesus Christ: "For by grace you have been saved *through faith;* and that not of yourselves, it is a gift of God; not as a result of works, that no one should boast" (Ephesians 2:8,9, NAS).

If a prayer was involved in your conversion experience, the prayer was not the actual means by which you received Christ; rather, it served as a verbal expression of your faith and as a deliberate invitation for Christ to come into your life.

How can you be filled with the Holy Spirit? Paul's letter to the Christians at Colossae tells us that we are filled with the Holy Spirit in the same way we received Christ — by faith. "As you therefore have received Christ Jesus the Lord, so walk in Him" (Colossians 2:6, NAS).

Prepare the "Throne"

Since faith is the means by which we can claim the fullness of the Holy Spirit, it is vital that our faith be sincere—the result of a heart that is genuinely prepared and willing and surrendered to God. I believe there are four important steps the Christian should take to ready the "throne" of his life for the Holy Spirit's control.

1. Be sure you are indeed a member of the Family.

Have you actually joined the Family of God by receiving Jesus Christ as your own personal Savior and Lord? If you have, you do not need to receive Him again, for He has not left you. You may have slipped into the state described earlier as the "carnal" man or woman, where Christ is in your life but He is not on the throne.

Perhaps you have believed in the existence of God and His Son and have tried to live an honest life, but you have never consciously committed your life to Him and invited Him to take up residence within you. Without this commitment of faith, you are the "natural" man or woman. Before you can be filled by the Spirit and enjoy His wonderful blessings, you must receive Christ.

If you are unsure that if you were to die today you would go to heaven, let me encourage you to turn to Appendix A, "Would You Like to Know God Personally?" This will help you understand and make the most important decision of your life.

2. You must sincerely desire to be directed and empowered by the Holy Spirit.

Again, God will not push Himself upon you if you are intent on going your own way. But if you genuinely long to live a life that honors Him, He will empower you to do so. Jesus promised, "Blessed are those who hunger and thirst for righteousness, for they shall be filled" (Matthew 5:6, NAS).

*3. You must be willing to present every area of your life
to God.*

> And so, dear brothers, I plead with you to give your
> bodies to God. Let them be a living sacrifice, holy – the
> kind he can accept . . . Don't copy the behavior and
> customs of this world, but be a new and different person
> with a fresh newness in all you do and think. Then you
> will learn from your own experience how his ways will
> really satisfy you (Romans 12:1,2).

In my years of ministry, I have observed that this issue
of total surrender is perhaps the greatest stumbling block
for Christians trying to live a fruitful life. We are willing to
commit most of ourselves to God, but our fleshly nature
seems bent on holding something back:

"Lord Jesus, I yield my whole life to You (but I'm going
to retain control of my finances, thank You)."

"Lord Jesus, fill me with Your Spirit (but You can't
possibly understand my work situation, so I'll continue
being critical of my boss)."

"Lord Jesus, I give You control of the throne of my life
(but please don't interfere when I fantasize about the opposite sex)."

"Lord Jesus, I give You my life (but I don't trust You
with my career)."

Do you see the problem with this attitude? We pray to
the "Lord Jesus," yet if He is not Lord *of all* He is not Lord
at all. He is an all-or-nothing Lord.

It is impossible to know the joy, excitement and adventure of the Spirit-filled life until we have made a full
surrender of every area of our lives to the Lordship of
Christ. If we are not willing to surrender every area of our
lives to His control, then He must respond, "Thanks, but
no thanks – I cannot share the throne with you. You are

not ready to be filled with My Spirit."

4. You must deal with any unconfessed sin in your life.

The psalmist wrote, "If I regard iniquity in my heart, the Lord will not hear me" (Psalm 66:18, NAS). This is a basic law of man's relationship with God. When we commit sin, which we all do, we virtually have climbed back up on the throne and told our Lord, "Move aside—I'll take charge for awhile." This is disobedience, and moves us out of fellowship with God. He does not hear the prayer of a sinful heart unless it is the prayer of confession.

The apostle John wrote, "If we say that we have no sin, we are deceiving ourselves. If we confess our sins, He is faithful and righteous to forgive us our sins and to cleanse us from all unrighteousness" (1 John 1:8,9, NAS).

So our final and perhaps most important step in preparing the throne for our Lord is to clear away the litter from our occupation of that throne—to confess and be cleansed from our sin.

It is not necessary to engage in long periods of anguished, morbid introspection, nor to seek an emotional experience as Ned did. Simply wait quietly before God, asking Him to reveal to you, through His Holy Spirit, any areas that are not right with Him.

- Have you offended a friend, and not asked his forgiveness?
- Have you violated a command of God's Word, and not asked His forgiveness?
- Have you lived in anxiety or worry? Are you cynical or critical? Negative in your outlook?
- Have you been unloving to others at home, work, church or elsewhere?
- Have you been dishonest in your finances or work

habits? Or disloyal to your employer?

● Have you dwelled on lustful thoughts?

● Have you failed to tell someone about Christ when the Holy Spirit was prompting you to do so?

● Have temporal pursuits (work, money, things, pleasure) dominated your thinking and lifestyle?

The original meaning of the word *confess* means "to agree with." So as the Holy Spirit brings specific sins to mind and you confess them to God, you are saying: (1) "God, I agree with You that these things I'm doing (list them specifically) are sinful"; (2) "I agree with You that Christ died on the cross for these sins"; and (3) "I repent—I consciously turn my mind and heart from my sins and toward obedience to You." You can now appropriate His forgiveness according to His promise in 1 John 1:9. If your sin offended or wronged another person, it is vital that you go to that person, confess the wrong, and make restitution.

Discover the Fullness of the Holy Spirit

Since God commands us to be filled with the Holy Spirit, we know it is His will for us to be filled. Further, He promises in 1 John 5:14,15 that if we pray according to His will, He will hear us and answer us. Right now, in faith that God keeps His promises, you can claim His fullness and He will fill you with His Spirit.

Remember that you are not filled through confession or prayer. You are filled by faith and by faith alone. However, confession is an essential preparatory step to "clean the throne" for the Holy Spirit's control and direction, and prayer is a way to consciously express your faith and surrender the throne to His control. Let me share with you a suggested prayer that may help you verbalize this commitment:

Dear Father, I need you. I acknowledge that I have been in control of my life, and as a result I have sinned against You. Thank You for forgiving my sins through Christ's death on the cross.

I now invite Christ to again take His place of authority on the throne of my life. Fill me with Your Holy Spirit as You commanded me to be filled, and as You promised in Your Word You would do if I ask in faith.

I pray this in the name of Jesus. As an expression of my faith, I now thank You for directing my life and for filling me with Your Holy Spirit.

If this suggested prayer expresses the desire of your heart, I encourage you to pray right now and, putting this prayer in your own words, trust God to fill you with His Holy Spirit.

Happiness Restored

When Janice attended one of our training conferences and learned about the personal ministry of the Holy Spirit, she understood for the first time the freedom and joy that could be hers as she applied this principle. "I had struggled for months with spiritual defeat," she reports. "I knew I should be spending time in God's Word and in prayer, but I just didn't care. God seemed distant to me. Church seemed like an empty formality. I even grew cynical and critical of my Christian friends, resenting their successes and happiness."

Janice had tried positive thinking, listening to upbeat music, smiling into a mirror and other strategies to lift herself out of the doldrums, all to no avail. That cloud of lethargy and cynicism stayed with her. Then, at the conference, she learned that her misery was the result of being out of fellowship with God because of unconfessed sin.

"The speaker challenged each of us to take a few moments with pen and pad in hand, asking God to reveal any unconfessed sin in our lives. 'No morbid introspection,' he warned us. 'Don't struggle to find sin—just let the Holy Spirit reveal anything that grieves Him or quenches your relationship with Him.'"

As Janice prayed for guidance, several items came to mind. She wrote on her pad:

critical, cynical spirit

resentment and bitterness toward my friends

"don't care" attitude

lack of prayer life or time in the Word

"The speaker told us to agree with God that these items were sin, then ask Him to forgive and cleanse us from those sins and retake the throne. When I did this, I felt a tremendous burden lift from me. I had been living all those months as a carnal Christian, in unconfessed sin, struggling to be a positive Christian—when all I needed to do was deal with the sin in my life.

"As the final part of this exercise, the speaker had us write 1 John 1:9 across the top of our pads:

If we confess our sins, He is faithful and righteous to forgive us our sins, and to cleanse us from all unrighteousness.

"In other words, since I had sincerely confessed my sins, I could bank on the fact that God had forgiven me and cleansed me. The speaker had us tear up the sheet of paper to drive home the fact that God had forgiven and forgotten our sins—and so could we!"

Janice had let unconfessed sin drag her down into the pit of despair. Unfortunately, I have found that this situation is all too common among Christians, as a vast majority admit that their lives do not measure up to the joy, freedom, power and purpose God promises in His Word. Like Janice, many of us allow our sins to stagnate for weeks, months or even years. *But we do not need to live this way!* Jesus promised us a full and abundant life if only we will trust and obey Him.

God wants us to deal with sin on a moment-by-moment basis.

He commands that we be filled, and His commands are not optional.

He promises to fill us if we prepare our hearts and sincerely trust Him to do so.

So when you genuinely yield your heart to the Lord, holding nothing back, He keeps His promise to retake the throne. Fellowship with Him is restored. You receive power to live His way. Your life takes on a renewed sense of love, joy and peace because He fills you with His love, joy and peace—as well as patience, kindness, goodness, faithfulness, gentleness and self-control (Galatians 5:22,23).

You have discovered the key to the vault—the Christian's secret of a life of purpose and power!

"Blessed are they who hunger and thirst after righteousness, for *they shall be filled.*"

FOR REFLECTION, DISCUSSION AND ACTION

1. Before you studied this chapter, how would you have described the process of being filled with the Spirit?

2. If a fellow Christian came to you and asked, "How can I be filled with the Holy Spirit?" what would you tell him?

3. Explain what is meant by the fact that we are filled with the Holy Spirit by faith.

4. Is there any part of your life that you have held back from the Lordship of Jesus Christ? If so, why? Why is it vital that we surrender every area to His control?

5. Explain in your own words why unconfessed sin is in-

compatible with the Spirit-filled life.

6. Just as Janice did, invest several minutes alone with a pad of paper, asking God to reveal through the Holy Spirit any unconfessed sins in your life. Write them down as the Holy Spirit brings them to your mind.

Then, agree with God that these items are sin and that you genuinely desire to live in a way that pleases Him. Ask God to forgive and cleanse you according to His promise in 1 John 1:9. (See the suggested prayer in this chapter).

Write out 1 John 1:9 across the top of the page: "If we confess our sins, He is faithful and righteous to forgive us our sins, and to cleanse us from all unrighteousness." Take a few moments to reflect on what this promise means to you right now.

Finally, to signify that God has forgiven you and forgotten your sin, tear up or burn your sheet of paper.

7. Picture in your mind the diagrams from the last chapter. Where is Christ right now? Are you filled with the Holy Spirit? Explain how you know.

6

"What Happens When I Sin?"

If a man is troubled about his sins, it is the work of the Spirit, for Satan never told him he was a sinner.
Dwight L. Moody

You *reacted in anger,* the thought seared the back of my mind. *You didn't take the time to listen to his concerns, and you were impatient. You hurt him.*

I like to plan as far in advance as possible, especially for key events. But occasionally I get so busy with the many details of our worldwide ministry that an important item slips through.

This was one of those occasions. With a key international conference just a couple of weeks away, I had just realized the need for a set of printed materials that would be of tremendous benefit to the conferees.

As I shared the urgency with the department director responsible for this need, he responded, "Bill, we're full up already. Two weeks just isn't enough time."

I became impatient. Couldn't my associate see that we are in a war for men's souls, that we must seize opportunities when they arise and not limit our efforts to 8-to-5 workdays? I made my point clear to him.

"But if we had had more notice . . ." he protested. "There just is no way we can squeeze in such a huge job with so little time. There's the writing, then the design and typesetting and artwork, then the printing—"

It seemed obvious that he did not share my burden for the upcoming event. I pressed my point. "Look, this is an important international conference," I said firmly, my voice rising. "And this is no time for 'business as usual.' Please find a way to finish this project in time for the conference, even if you have to work around the clock."

I could tell my colleague was frustrated. But I reasoned, *We need those printed materials. Whatever it takes, we need them.*

Within a few moments after our conversation, I sensed the conviction of the Holy Spirit. Yes, even in our well-intended service of the Lord, we can stumble—and in the name of godliness I had offended a dear brother in Christ. I had failed to give him and his staff the benefit of the doubt—failed to take into account the tough workload they already were facing each day. Instead of asking him to think through the possibilities with me and helping him rearrange his priorities to accommodate the new task, I had virtually ordered him to get the project done and shown little appreciation for the many late evenings his team was already devoting to their work. I had reacted impatiently rather than in a spirit of love, understanding and teamwork.

The Choice

At this point I had a choice to make.

On the one hand, I could let it go. After all, doesn't the head of a large organization have the right to ramrod projects through when necessary? Didn't the end (the strategic international conference) justify the means (get the job done no matter what it takes)? And didn't my associate's hesitant attitude warrant a stern talking-to about the urgency of the hour?

By all human standards, I probably could have justified letting the incident go. But deep inside I would have been restless and uncomfortable as the Holy Spirit continued to point out the sin to me, and God would not have blessed my future efforts on His behalf as long as this sin remained unconfessed. On top of that, several of my dear co-workers would have continued to hurt as a result of my callous attitude.

On the other hand, I could deal with the problem by taking scriptural action to clear the slate. The unrest in my conscience was the Holy Spirit cross-examining me as I tried to rationalize my behavior. What I had thought was forceful leadership, He was identifying as the sins of impatience and unjustifiable anger.

I knew that taking scriptural action was the only choice I could make that would please my Lord. I confessed my sin to Him and appropriated His forgiveness.

Then came the toughest part.

I drove down to the office complex where my associate and his team were located, and asked their forgiveness. We cried and laughed and prayed together, sensing a fresh outpouring of God's love in our midst. Then we talked through our mutual needs and found a way—as teammates—to rearrange priorities and accomplish the task—on time!

The Only Choice

Whenever a Christian stumbles and sins, he faces a similar choice. He can let it go, in which case he will continue to be troubled by spiritual unrest and ineffectiveness; or he can make things right with God and others and clean the slate.

I can testify from firsthand experience that, while making things right with God and others can be humbling, it is the only choice for those who want to live in the mainstream of God's blessings. Unconfessed sin breaks off fellowship with the Savior, resulting in spiritual impotence and unhappiness. David indicated in Psalms 32 and 51 that unconfessed sin can even lead to actual physical illness and other problems as guilt depletes the spiritual and psychological strength that helps keep the body well. (Of course, this is not to say that every time a Christian becomes ill it is due to unconfessed sin. It would be interesting, though, if we could learn just how many of our illnesses originate in this way.)

On the other hand, confession, forgiveness and restitution restore fellowship with God, cleanse us of the guilt of our sin, and open the door once again for the Holy Spirit to empower us.

I call this process "Spiritual Breathing." You won't find these words in the Bible, for Spiritual Breathing is simply an illustration to help us remember what to do to make things right with God. It is the act of keeping Christ on the throne of your life by confessing sin immediately, whenever the Holy Spirit convicts you, and claiming, by faith, the continued direction and control of the Holy Spirit for your life.

Though simple, Spiritual Breathing is not to be taken lightly. It is an act that requires a genuine desire to live according to God's Word.

I believe it is the most important principle I can share with my fellow Christians. In fact, it is so crucial to a joyful, fruitful life that it has become a major emphasis of our ministry. Literally thousands of Christians who have put this principle to work have reported that it has "completely changed" their lives and helped them to realize what "walking in the Spirit" is really all about.

One nationally known minister, who had pastored a thriving church for decades, called me a few weeks after he had heard me teach a seminar on Spiritual Breathing. "For the first time in my ministry," he confided, "I can help my people understand how the Holy Spirit works in us and how to deal with sin. Thank you for making it clear for me."

Recently, a highly respected Christian leader stood before a group of Christian peers and held up my book *The Holy Spirit: The Key to Supernatural Living.* "The principles explained in this book have changed my life," he exclaimed. "Now, at last, I understand what being filled with the Spirit really involves."

I cannot take any credit, for Spiritual Breathing is just a modern-day picture to help us apply what is already in God's Word. But I rejoice whenever a fellow believer grasps the principle and uses it to help him keep Christ on the throne of his life. As you practice Spiritual Breathing in your own daily walk, I am convinced you will agree that it is one of the most important lessons you will learn about successful Christian living.

How Spiritual Breathing Works

In order to stay physically healthy, we must exhale to cleanse the waste air from our systems (carbon dioxide) and then inhale to replenish the good air (oxygen). In similar fashion, Christians need to "breathe spiritually" to stay spiritually healthy. The moment the Holy Spirit convicts us of sin, we should "exhale" by confessing that sin to God. Let's say we have entertained a lustful fantasy toward another person. An appropriate prayer might go like this:

> Lord Jesus, I have sinned against You. You have designed me to enjoy a healthy, fulfilling sexuality with my spouse, but I have lusted after another person. I acknowledge that this is wrong and displeasing to You. I repent of this sin, and ask You to give me strength to obey You and resist Satan in this area.

After exhaling the impure, we can "inhale" the pure. This involves two important acknowledgments: (1) We receive God's forgiveness and cleansing; and (2) we appropriate (take into our personal possession) the fullness of the Holy Spirit.

How do we know God will forgive, cleanse and fill us? First, we know that being filled with the Holy Spirit is His will, for He has so commanded in Ephesians 5:18. Second, He promised in 1 John 5:14,15 that when we pray according to His will, He will grant our request. Third, He promised in 1 John 1:9 that if we confess our sins, He will forgive our sins and cleanse us of all unrighteousness. When we sincerely return the throne of our life to Him, we can know *by faith in the promises of His Word* that He will resume His rightful position on that throne. Our prayer can continue:

> Thank You for forgiving me for my sin through Your death on the cross, and for cleansing me of this sin. I again give You control of the throne of my life, and ask You to guide me away from those things which are displeasing to You. By faith, I claim the fullness, direction and power of Your Holy Spirit.

If done with a genuine desire to please God and achieve victory in this area of life, Spiritual Breathing is all it takes to make things right between you and your heavenly

Father, and you can once again be filled with the Spirit. You have fulfilled the requirement of 1 John 1:9 by acknowledging and repenting of your sin; God has fulfilled His promise to forgive, cleanse and fill you with His Holy Spirit.

No further payment is due! The account is paid in full! Fellowship with God is restored, guilt is washed away, and the sin does not linger to deteriorate into carnality. You are free to move forward in your walk with Jesus Christ.

How Often Should We Confess?

As Christians learn this important principle, some ask, "How often do I need to breathe spiritually?" The answer is, "As often as you sin!" As different situations arise, you may find that you have to breathe spiritually several times in one day. At other times, especially as you walk closely with God, you may not sin for several days, weeks or months. The important thing is to listen to the Holy Spirit when He convicts you of sin, and to take action to restore fellowship with God through confession, acceptance of His forgiveness, and appropriation of the Holy Spirit's power by faith.

The tangible benefit of keeping accounts short with God is that you allow Him to cleanse you of the impurity of sin before it can desensitize you to His guidance. As you deal honestly with sin, you will learn how to anticipate those temptations that are likely to be a stumbling block for you. You will begin to develop the strength and resolve to respond as Jesus would when that temptation comes along in the future.

License to Sin?

A cautionary note is in order at this point. Some immature Christians might look at 1 John 1:9 and Spiritual Breathing with the attitude that "if forgiveness is assured,

I can go ahead and sin. I can just clear the slate with God later."

To believe such, and to act upon it, is to presume upon God's grace and cheapen the ultimate sacrifice He made by sending His Son to die on the cross for us. He expects obedience, not just in our actions but in our heart's attitude. The apostle John addressed this issue clearly in his first letter:

> And how can we be sure that we belong to Him? By looking within ourselves: are we really trying to do what He wants us to? Someone may say, "I am a Christian; I am on my way to heaven; I belong to Christ." But if he doesn't do what Christ tells him to, he is a liar.

> But those who do what Christ tells them to will learn to love God more and more. That is the way to know whether or not you are a Christian. Anyone who says he is a Christian should live as Christ did (1 John 2:3-6).

The resounding message from God's Word is that if one does not have a genuine, heart-felt desire to please God in all things, it is possible that he never made a sincere commitment to God in the first place, never actually experienced the new birth, and thus cannot call himself a Christian. Harsh words, but they spell out God's expectation of our obedience.

When the scribes and Pharisees brought an adulterous woman to Jesus, He saw repentance in her spirit and forgave her of her sin. But He also said, "Go your way. From now on sin no more" (John 8:11). His forgiveness came readily; yet His grace did not give her license to continue her adulterous ways. He expected from her a serious commitment to change.

God's standard is nothing short of sinlessness. Though only one person, our Lord Jesus, has achieved that standard, our goal and inner desire must be to please God and obey Him in all things. As we already observed in John 14:21, our obedience (both in our actions and in our heart's desires) is a prime indicator of our love for God. Therefore, the Christian walk does not allow for the theory that God's grace gives us a license to sin.

In addition, we must remember that even though God forgives us when we confess sin, He always disciplines the disobedient. When we are truly repentant He will wash away the sin, but He lets us live with the consequences of our sin. God forgave the repentant King David, but David paid the price for the rest of his life for his sins of adultery and murder. God will forgive us if we truly repent of indulgence in pornography, but the images of what we have seen will continue to burn in our minds for years to come. He will forgive us for being rude to another person, but He does not magically heal the relationship we have harmed—we have to work to restore that relationship ourselves.

Fortunately, God is a realist. He knows that even though we may resolve not to sin, the battle continues to rage between Flesh and Spirit and we most likely *will* sin. "Yes, all have sinned," Paul wrote to the Christians in Rome. "All fall short of God's glorious ideal" (Romans 3:23).

That is why He sent Jesus Christ to pay the penalty, and why He extends forgiveness and cleansing for sin if we will only confess and repent of that sin to Him. It is why we can "breathe spiritually" and make things right within just a few moments whenever the Holy Spirit whispers that we have displeased God.

When Do I Become Carnal?

It is important to clarify that the Christian who sins does not necessarily become "carnal" (see 1 Corinthians 3:1-3 and Chapter 4 of this book) the moment he sins. And if the Christian exercises Spiritual Breathing upon being convicted of that sin, he has not necessarily lapsed into a state of carnality between the moment of sin and the moment of confession.

When Paul wrote of the carnal man, he was writing to a group of Christians who regularly bickered with one another. "When you are jealous of one another and divide up in quarreling groups, doesn't that prove you are still babies, wanting your own way?" he asked the Corinthians. "In fact, you are acting like people who don't belong to the Lord at all" (1 Corinthians 3:3). In other words, they had allowed sin to be an ongoing problem in their lives. They had taken control of the throne, and had continued their sinful ways without confessing their sin, appropriating God's forgiveness, and living in harmony with one another.

This is when sin becomes carnality. The Christian becomes carnal when he ceases to believe and act upon the promises and commands of God in faith. He has neglected to breathe spiritually when the Holy Spirit has prompted him to do so. He hopes that "time will heal all wounds," that if he ignores it or gets active in good works, the sin will go away. The usual result, however, is just the opposite. One sin accumulates upon another, growing into a wretched garbage pile of the soul. This pile of unconfessed sin then leads to an even more rebellious spirit—a spirit that is more desensitized to the urgings of the Holy Spirit— which in turn negates the Christian's inner joy and outward testimony.

No wonder Paul calls this individual a "baby"!

The Secret

This brings us right back to the key to a successful, happy, consistent Christian life. The secret is simply to keep Christ on the throne of your life by keeping short accounts with God. How do you keep short accounts? Through Spiritual Breathing. The moment the Holy Spirit pricks your conscience, exhale the "polluted air" by confessing and sincerely repenting of your sin to God. Then inhale the fresh morning breeze of His forgiveness, cleansing and fullness by acknowledging your faith in His promise in 1 John 1:9 to forgive and cleanse you of all unrighteousness.

He *will* forgive you and cleanse you! He *will*, upon your invitation, take control of the throne of your life again and fill you with the power and purpose of His Holy Spirit. You will be free to enjoy life, to love others and to serve Him with all your heart.

The Importance of Restitution

While Spiritual Breathing restores our fellowship with the Lord Jesus Christ, it is important to emphasize that if our sin has offended or wronged another person, the process is incomplete until we also have confessed our sin to the wronged individual and asked his forgiveness. As I have already admitted from personal experience, this is often the hardest part of the entire process.

Not long ago John, a Christian in his mid-thirties, came to me for counsel. He told how, several months earlier, he had taken home some merchandise from his employer. He knew he had been wrong, and he had not removed any items since. But even now, every time John went before God in prayer his mind was filled with those items he had stolen.

"I really want to be a man of God," he told me. "I've confessed my sin, but I still feel dirty about what I've done."

I took a Bible from the coffee table, opened it to Matthew 5:23, and we read aloud our Lord's words:

"So if you are standing before the altar in the Temple, offering a sacrifice to God, and suddenly remem-

ber that a friend has something against you, leave your
sacrifice there beside the altar and go and apologize and
be reconciled to him, and then come and offer your
sacrifice to God."

A look of conviction crossed John's face as I asked him,
"What is Jesus saying you need to do?"

The obvious answer was painful for him. "But if I go
to my boss and admit what I've done, he could fire me."

"Yes," I acknowledged, "that's a possibility. But if you
want to be a man of God, the Scriptures leave you no choice.
You must try to make things right with your employer."

"But I have a family—a mortgage . . ." John's voice
trailed off as he realized what he needed to do, and what
the possible consequences were.

John went to his employer the next day, confessed his
theft, asked for forgiveness, and offered to work without
pay until restitution was made. Then he sat back and held
his breath.

The employer was taken aback at the confession. After
a few awkward moments, he expressed appreciation for
John's honesty and arranged to withhold an amount from
each paycheck until the debt was paid. "It was the toughest
thing I've ever had to do in my life," John reported back to
me. "I had confessed my sin to God, but according to Matthew 5:23 I also needed to make things right with my boss.
It wasn't until I obeyed God's Word and made restitution
that He set me free from the misery of what I had done."

There is no exhilaration quite like the feeling you get
when you have made things right with God and your fellow
man. It's like taking a hot shower after an arduous day's
work—the sweat and dirt and aches and fatigue ease away
and you feel refreshed, relaxed, at peace. Spiritual Breathing cleanses away the grime that has come between you and
God and replaces it with the inner sparkle of knowing that

all is right with Him.

"It Works!"

Carl and Jan, whom you met in Chapter 2, can vouch
for how well this works. As you will recall, Carl had a critical spirit and his beautiful wife Jan bore the brunt of her
husband's insensitivity. Jan reports that, while Carl "still
slips occasionally, he has gotten much, much better. He's
actually fun to be around!"

Carl picks up the story. "I know that a critical spirit
is sin, and to hurt another person with my harsh words is
sin. And since I honestly want to please God, He lets me
know [through the prompting of the Holy Spirit] when I
have spoken unfairly to Jan.

"And this is where Spiritual Breathing has made all
the difference in the world. Out with the bad air, in with
the good air. I agree with God about the sin and express
again my deep desire to change, then appropriate His forgiveness and cleansing from that sin. With God, the issue
is history.

"But the act of Spiritual Breathing makes something
else obvious to me. I've made things right with God, but I
still need to make things right with the woman I love. I
need to 'breathe relationally' with Jan by acknowledging
to her that I was wrong and asking her to forgive me. For
some reason, this is more humbling to me than confessing
to God, but I know I have to do it to 'restore fellowship'
with my longsuffering wife.

"The result? Instead of a fight lingering for days or
weeks, we've resolved it within minutes. I've kept short accounts with God and with Jan as well. I'm happier in my
relationship with God, and our marriage has made a 180-
degree turn for the better."

As Carl tells his story, the beaming smile on Jan's face

verifies what he says. "Keep telling everyone about Spiritual Breathing," she says to me excitedly. "It works!"

Indeed, it does—and you can put Spiritual Breathing to work in *your* life, right now. Let me encourage you to make a solemn commitment to our Lord: that from this moment forward, you will seek to keep Christ on the throne of your life by keeping short accounts with God. Commit to Him that you will breathe spiritually whenever the Holy Spirit points out a sin in your life.

As you follow through on this commitment, you will be walking in God's will by obeying His command to be continually filled, controlled and empowered by the Spirit. You will be free from the guilt and misery of sin. You will enjoy the peace of knowing that all is right between you and your heavenly Father.

In fact, God's Word promises nine specific benefits of a Spirit-filled life. We'll identify them, and see what they mean to you, as our journey continues.

FOR REFLECTION, DISCUSSION AND ACTION

1. Why do you think Dwight L. Moody wrote (in the statement at the beginning of this chapter) "for Satan never told him he was a sinner"?

2. Whenever you sense the Holy Spirit's conviction regarding sin, you have a choice: Let it go, or make things right with God and others. From the human perspective, which choice is easier? Why?

3. Give several reasons why it is essential that we keep short accounts with God. Then, give several reasons why we should seek the forgiveness of others when we have offended them.

4. If a Christian friend came to you and asked, "What is the secret to living a successful Christian life?" what would

you say to help him?

5. Why, despite God's generous grace, does He place such a strong emphasis on our inner and outward obedience to Him?

6. Read and reflect on Psalms 32 and 51. What modern-day lessons are to be found in David's writings?

7. Commit today to keeping short accounts with God by making Spiritual Breathing a part of your life.

7

Divine Pleasures of the Spirit-filled Walk

*"I came that they might have life, and might
have it abundantly."*

*Jesus Christ
John 10:10*

Bill, you're unbelievable," a friend once told me.
"Doesn't anything ever get you down?"

I have a reputation for being an optimist. Oh, I have
my moments like everyone else when I am tempted and discouraged, but one of the greatest lessons I have learned
through the years is to give praise to my Lord and Savior
in all things—in the trials as well as the triumphs.

And I do have my fair share of trials. Frankly, the
fleshly part of me would get discouraged—sometimes
upset—in the face of adversity. Without Christ on the
throne of my life, my outlook and demeanor would be any-

thing but cheerful. But I have discovered that the more I praise my heavenly Father, meditate on His wonderful Word, walk in the power of the Holy Spirit and talk with others about Jesus, the less my natural side comes through. The Holy Spirit overrules my natural tendencies and fills me with optimism, joy and peace.

Just a few days ago an assistant brought me news of a problem that had arisen in our preparations for New Life 2000^{SM} (a major worldwide evangelistic campaign we are spearheading in cooperation with thousands of churches and Christian organizations). Any undertaking this large encounters snags, and this particular problem was neither the first nor the last.

But upon hearing the news, my first reaction was to praise God that He is bigger than any problems I might ever encounter ("Is anything too difficult for the LORD?" God asked Abraham rhetorically in Genesis 18:14). Through four decades of ministry He has answered our prayers and met our needs so many times that I have learned to place my total confidence in Him—even when a solution seems humanly impossible.

In this situation, the act of praising His glorious name moved our focus off the problem and onto the problem-solver, our powerful Savior. We then asked Him for wisdom, and that His Holy Spirit would guide us as we discussed possible solutions.

As I confessed to you in the opening of the last chapter, I don't respond this way every time—my sinful nature can still cause trouble. But as I have grown in the Lord and allowed Him to guide me through His Spirit, His supernatural joy and peace have become more and more a part of me. I don't have to struggle to be joyful and calm in my own strength; the Spirit of God pours out an ample supply of optimism from within so that generally my first reaction to adversity is one of genuine joy and peace.

The Fruit of the Spirit

Joy is just one of the divine pleasures of the Spirit-directed walk, for as we keep Christ on the throne, we reap the benefits of the omnipotent, caring God who is at work conforming us to the image of Jesus Christ.

In Galatians 5:22,23, the apostle Paul lists nine specific benefits that grow within when we are filled with the Spirit. He calls them "fruit of the Spirit," meaning that they are a natural outgrowth of our intimacy with the Lord Jesus Christ. As we walk in Him and grow in Him, He produces these qualities within us:

love

joy

peace

patience

kindness

goodness

faithfulness

gentleness

self-control

That's quite a list! My good friend Dan Benson, in his book *The Total Man,* aptly calls it "The Ultimate New Year's Resolution List," for these are the very inner qualities men and women have striven for since time began. Who *wouldn't* want to be more loving, joyful, peaceful, patient, kind, good, faithful, gentle and self-disciplined?

The fruit of the Spirit are not only benefits of the Spirit-filled life, they are *pleasures* of the Spirit-filled life as well. It brings pleasure—to you and to others and to God—when you genuinely love Him and your fellow man. It brings pleasure—to you and to others and to God—when joy radiates from your countenance. That is why it is impossible for the Spirit-directed walk to be one of misery. God pours His pleasurable attributes into us so that they might flow out into our attitudes and actions.

Realistically, because we are still human, we do not become experts in these nine pleasures right away. Like any fruit on a growing plant or tree, they take time and are subject to the inner condition of the plant itself. In a drought of carnality, the fruit can shrivel on our branches; but in the moist, verdant spiritual state the fruit will grow and prosper.

In a moment, we're going to take a closer look at these pleasures and what they mean to us in the daily challenges we might encounter. But first it's important that we know why Paul wrote about the fruit of the Spirit. It all started when he learned of one group of Christians who had found a sure way to be miserable.

Legalism vs. Liberty

Paul penned his letter to the Galatians in response to dangerous false teaching that was being spread by certain Jewish Christians. The Judaizers, clinging to the laws of Moses, were teaching that God's grace was not sufficient for man's salvation—that men and women also needed to keep all the Old Testament rules and regulations in order to earn their way to heaven.

The controversy boiled down to the doctrine of legalism versus the doctrine of liberty. The Judaizers contended that it was good works and the keeping of all the rules that resulted in eternal salvation. Paul, through the guidance of the Holy Spirit, taught: "It is by grace you have been saved, through faith—and this not from yourselves, it is the gift of God—not by works, so that no one can boast" (Ephesians 2:8,9, NIV).

The situation became so heated that the Judaizers

began calling Paul names and urging Christians not to listen to him. So Paul set the record straight with this powerful letter defending the doctrine of salvation by faith alone. His premise:

> The Jewish laws were our teacher and guide until Christ came to give us right standing with God through our faith. But now that Christ has come, we don't need those laws any longer to guard us and lead us to him. For we are all children of God through faith in Jesus Christ (Galatians 3:24-26).

Paul also noticed that the Christians living by legalism weren't really very happy. Their focus on keeping the rules instead of on knowing Jesus Christ personally robbed them of their joy. They had left their first love:

> And now that you have found God (or should I say, now that God has found you) how can it be that you want to go back again and become slaves once more to another poor, weak, useless religion of trying to get to heaven by obeying God's laws? . . . Where is that happy spirit that we felt together then? (Galatians 4:9,15)

One of the major heresies of all time is the doctrine of legalism. Unfortunately, many Christians today still follow this doctrine. They believe that, in addition to receiving Christ as Savior and Lord, their ultimate salvation and favor with God depends on how they keep a long list of *gotto's* and *can't-do's*. Paul emphasized that the focal point of Christianity is not the keeping of these standards but rather the person of the Lord Jesus Christ.

Have you ever known a Christian who subscribed to the doctrine of legalism? Was that person truly happy?

It is impossible for a Christian to have the joy of Christ in his heart if he lives this way. Instead of the fruit of the Spirit, self-righteous bitterness wells up and spews out of him in the form of a judgmental, negative, defeatist attitude. Such a Christian isn't much fun to be around.

The Secret to Liberty: The Holy Spirit

"I advise you to obey only the Holy Spirit's instructions," Paul urged the Galatian believers. "He will tell you where to go and what to do, and then you won't always be doing the wrong things your evil nature wants you to" (5:16).

As a former devout Jew himself, Paul knew from experience that legalism only leads to frustration and unhappiness.

So he knew what he was talking about when he wrote the core message of his forceful letter: *"When you are guided by the Holy Spirit you need no longer force yourself to obey Jewish laws"* (Galatians 5:18).

There it is again, the secret to fulfillment, happiness, and liberty in Christ: the Holy Spirit. With Him on the throne of our lives, we need not focus on the *got-to's* and *can't-do's* of religiosity. Instead, we can focus on knowing God, enjoying Him, and sharing His love with the world around us. We can proclaim with the apostle Paul, "Christ has made us free!"

So Paul set the stage beautifully for Galatians 5:18, that joyous list of the character qualities that will grow in our lives when we walk in the liberty and power of the Holy Spirit. "But when the Holy Spirit controls our lives," he writes, "he will produce this kind of fruit in us . . ."

Love

Is there someone at work, or in your church or neighborhood, whom you have trouble loving?

Our Lord Jesus gave love the highest priority. "I am giving a new commandment to you now—love each other just as much as I love you," He instructed the disciples in John 13:34. The apostle Paul carried on the Master's teaching by writing, "For the whole Law can be summed up in this one command: 'Love others as you love yourself'" (Galatians 5:14).

In the time of Jesus and Paul, there were three Greek words which we now translate into our English word "love:" *Eros, phileo,* and *agape.*

Eros suggests sensual titillation; it conveys the idea that "I love you because you excite my sexual desires." We get our modern term *erotic* from this Greek word.

Phileo is used to depict the love between friends or relatives. It suggests that "I love you because our friendship or family ties make you deserve to be loved."

Agape is God's supernatural, unconditional love—the love He showed an undeserving world when He sent His Son to die on the cross for our sins. *Agape* is love because of the inner character of the person who is doing the loving, rather than because the object of that devotion is worthy. It is often love "in spite of" rather than love "because." *Agape* says, "I love you unconditionally—in spite of your sin or your attitude, or regardless of whether you love me."

It is *agape* that both our Lord Jesus Christ and the apostle Paul were talking about when they commanded Christians to love one another. Paul recognized that unconditional love was such an important pleasure in the Christian walk that he devoted an entire chapter to it: 1 Corinthians 13. In this classic, poetic masterpiece, he emphasizes the truth that *agape* must be our greatest aim; that no matter what else we do for God or others, our actions are of no value unless we do them from the wellsprings of God's love.

> If I had the gift of being able to speak in other languages without learning them, and could speak in every

language there is in all of heaven and earth, but didn't
love others, I would only be making noise.

If I had the gift of prophecy and knew all about what
is going to happen in the future, knew everything about
everything, but didn't love others, what good would it do?

. . . If I gave everything I have to poor people, and
if I were burned alive for preaching the gospel but didn't
love others, it would be of no value whatever (1 Corinthians 13:1-3).

But God does not leave us to manufacture *agape* in our
own strength. Our source of unconditional love is the Holy
Spirit. Sherwood Eliot Wirt, in his beautiful modern-day
classic *The Inner Life of the Believer,* shares a simple yet
fascinating syllogism about the role of the Holy Spirit in
helping us love others:

God is love.

The Holy Spirit is God.

Therefore: The Holy Spirit is love.

Since the Holy Spirit is love, as long as we allow Him
to remain on the throne of our lives we will have both the
character and the conduit to love others unconditionally.
We can choose to love a family member when he is behav-
ing badly; we can choose to love a co-worker in spite of his
uncooperative attitude; we can choose to love a fellow
churchgoer even when he spreads rumors about us; we can
choose to love a neighbor even if he revs his Harley-David-
son at 6 o'clock on a Saturday morning.

---

*CHECKPOINT: Do I genuinely love others today . . .
in spite of how they act toward me?* If so, it's a good indication that my Lord is on the throne. If I'm not experiencing the pleasure of loving others
unconditionally, it could indicate that I need to deal
with some unconfessed sin.

Joy

"Joy is the serious business of heaven," wrote C. S. Lewis. And isn't that really what Christianity is all about — bringing joy to our world?

Joy goes far deeper than mere happiness. It is an inner gladness that puts a song in our hearts in bad times as well as good. Joy comes from the ecstasy of knowing God personally and knowing His plan for our time and eternity; therefore it is not dependent on the whims of circumstance or the human tragedies that beset us.

A few years ago, my friends Glen and Marilyn Heavilin went through the deepest of anguish when their all-American seventeen-year-old son Nathan was killed by a drunk driver. In earlier years, the Heavilins had lost two other sons in infancy, which made this latest tragedy even more devastating. As Glen and Marilyn suffered through the grief and heartache of Nathan's death, they and their friends shed tears of mourning, shock and loss. Yet, despite the wrenching pain of their experience, their friends noticed an inner quality in the Heavilins that somehow helped bring an undercurrent of strength and hope to the tragic situation.

That inner quality was joy — provided by the Holy Spirit. Of course, this wonderful couple could not be *happy* about their son's death. But in spite of the nightmare of shock and shattered dreams, they were able, through their tears and heartbreak, to acknowledge Nathan's presence in the arms of their loving Lord . . . to acknowledge that even though they couldn't understand God's sovereignty in this circumstance, He indeed is in control.

The Holy Spirit came through to bring praise in the midst of pain, joy in the midst of sadness. In the years since, Glen and Marilyn have shared the experience with thousands of readers through Marilyn's two excellent books, *Roses in December* and *December's Song*. In speaking engagements, as well as through her books, she is bringing comfort to others who grieve and she is pointing them to Jesus Christ.

If the Holy Spirit can bring joy in the midst of life's deepest adversities, He also can bring joy amidst any of our other circumstances. "Always be full of joy in the Lord," Paul wrote—from a prison cell. "I say it again, rejoice!" (Philippians 4:4).

CHECKPOINT: Am I experiencing genuine joy in my heart today? Is there a song of praise to the Lord, in spite of what's going on around me? Do I honor God with a joyful countenance? If so, the Holy Spirit is working His good pleasure within me. If not, I am not honoring my Lord with sullenness. It could be that some Spiritual Breathing is in order.

Peace

"God takes life's broken pieces and gives us unbroken peace," wrote Wilbert Donald Gough.

Peace is a sense of inner calm and security in the midst of the storms that rage around us. It is a quiet confidence that, since God is in control, we have nothing to fear.

George, a Christian for almost three decades, is an anxious sort. He thinks Murphy's Law was written just for him. George worries about his current bills and about next month's bills. He worries about what's happening at the office today and what might happen tomorrow. Whenever someone rejoices that a glass is half-full, he points out that on the other hand, the glass is half-empty. Mark Twain must have had George in mind when he wrote, "I have endured many trials in life, most of which never happened."

Sheila, another believer, radiates peace. A diligent

worker, she has just as many problems and challenges as George (except for his imagined ones) but you'll usually catch her with a contagious smile on her lips, a sparkle in her eye, and an attitude which seems to say, *Do your very best, then relax. All is secure, for God is in charge here.*

You've known Christians like George and Sheila. Who do you think enjoys life more? Who is more fun to work with? Which way of life do you believe presents the best Christian witness to the world?

While exercise, rest and relaxation can help restore a sense of inner calm to our spirits, such activities are temporary relaxants at best. The true and lasting source of peace, we are told in God's Word, is the Holy Spirit. Jesus promised, "I am leaving you with a gift — peace of mind and heart! And the peace I give isn't fragile like the peace the world gives. So don't be troubled and afraid" (John 14:27).

CHECKPOINT: Do I feel peace within? Am I anxious over a relationship, a financial problem, a situation at work? Do I worry about things over which I have no control? If I am at peace, it's a good indication that I am walking in the fullness of the Holy Spirit. But if I am anxious, I am not glorifying God. I need to make sure Christ is on the throne, then cast my burdens upon Him.

Patience

Patience is the ability to put the rights and needs of someone else before our own; the ability to wait calmly for something we expect.

Without patience, we can thwart the will of God by acting presumptuously. Impatience also can destroy relationships, because it always puts self ahead of others.

Denise is a model of patience in action. When her

beloved husband Fred became bedridden with terminal stomach cancer, she stayed with him day and night. For several months until his death, she spoon-fed him, changed his soiled clothing, read to him, sang to him, and tried to soothe the agonizing pain. Never once did she complain about how his illness had virtually put her life on "hold." Denise completely placed Fred's needs before her own as her patience — born of love — ministered to him.

As the Holy Spirit filled her with the pleasure of patience, she in turn filled her husband's final days with love. Denise admits that her natural tendency would have been to complain about her situation and to try to escape the horror of watching her life's partner shrivel away. "But the Lord gave me the desire, and the strength, to minister to Fred even though he had nothing to give to me," Denise says. "The Holy Spirit supplied me with the patience to take care of him to the very end."

Patience is a pleasure in many other areas as well. It is a law of life that anytime you wish to do something important, at least three or four other people will form a line in front of you wanting to do the same thing. You can fuss and be miserable, or you can be patient and find a pleasant way to invest the waiting time.

Children have a way of testing the genuineness of our patience. They can throw tantrums worthy of Academy Awards, spill Coke on the family room carpet and leave it there for you to clean up, or wait until 9:30 tonight to announce that they need a giraffe costume for tomorrow's skit at school.

Paul wrote to the Romans that God is the source of patience: "May God who gives patience, steadiness, and encouragement help you to live in complete harmony with each other — each with the attitude of Christ toward the other" (Romans 15:5).

CHECKPOINT: Am I a patient person today? Am I free to relax while I put the needs of others before my own? If I find myself getting impatient over the big or little things of life, it might be time for a "throne check." I'll stop right now and ask God to reveal any impatience in my life.

Kindness

"One kind word can warm three winter months," says a Japanese proverb.

Kind words indeed warm the human spirit. Kindness is literally love in action, showing genuine friendship to others by regarding them as important in God's sight and worthy of dignity and respect. It involves treating others with courtesy, lending encouragement, and freely offering yourself or your resources to help a person in need, no strings attached.

The apostle Paul wrote, "We try to live in such a way that no one will be offended or kept back from finding the Lord by the way we act, so that no one can find fault with us and blame it on the Lord" (2 Corinthians 6:3).

In the book of Proverbs, we read that kindness is a prime quality of a virtuous woman: "When she speaks, her words are wise, and kindness is the rule for everything she says" (Proverbs 31:26). Men, these virtues are for us, too!

Jim has discovered the pleasure of kindness. He makes a special effort to brighten someone's day with an unexpected kind word or gesture. He'll say to a busy waitress, "I really appreciate your smile . . . you've made my lunch time even more enjoyable." At work, he frequently expresses appreciation to others for the jobs they do. With his neighbors, he is quick to lend a helping hand or offer encouragement.

Imagine the impact Christians could have on the world if kindness were the rule in all we do!

CHECKPOINT: Does kindness flow from me today? Do I consistently treat others, including my immediate family, with courtesy and respect? Am I quick to lend a kind or encouraging word, or a hand to someone in need? If kindness isn't flowing naturally from within, it may indicate a need to make things right with God and with others.

Goodness

Someone has said that goodness is not so much the outward thing we do as it is the inward thing we are. It is being filled with the highest ethical and moral standards and a genuine inner desire to live as God wants us to live. Quite literally, goodness means "to be like God."

Sir Francis Bacon said, "Of all virtues and dignities of the mind, goodness is the greatest, being the character of the Deity; and without it, man is a busy, mischievous, wretched thing."

I must agree. As we have already seen, the natural man has an evil nature and without God he will always gravitate toward the "me-first" self-gratifications of life. Contrary to the teachings of the New Age movement, God's Word clearly tells us that man cannot be like God by his own doing; goodness only comes about through the indwelling Holy Spirit.

A few years ago I met an intelligent man who had been a militant atheist all his life. In fact, Harold had dedicated himself to slandering Christianity and "proving" our faith to be a big fairy tale. By his own admission, he had been hostile to the point of obnoxious.

Then something happened — Harold received Christ!

The power of God's Word broke through to him, and he dedicated his life to Jesus Christ. "My insecurity and hostility left me," he recalled excitedly. "God has replaced my anger and hate with love."

That's the power of the Holy Spirit at work, transforming "badness" to goodness. Harold now has a genuine desire to think and live as God wants him to.

CHECKPOINT: Am I motivated by goodness today? Do I genuinely want to be, think and act like Jesus? As I grow in Christ and walk in His Spirit, goodness will become more and more natural for me. If I haven't had a genuine desire to be Christlike, it is an indication that I have allowed my fleshly nature to control me. It's time to "turn the dial" and yield to the Spirit.

Faithfulness

Faithfulness means staying steadfast and loyal to a person or cause and working diligently for the dream that person or cause is seeking to fulfill. It is the process of "hanging in there" through both the good and bad times.

In a marriage, we regard a spouse as "faithful" when he forsakes all others and builds the sexual/emotional bond exclusively with his marriage partner. In a friendship, we consider someone faithful if he is always there when we need a listening ear or a shoulder to cry on.

Faithfulness in our human relationships is one important pleasure the Holy Spirit produces within us. The other side of the coin is faithfulness in our relationship with God. If we invite Him to reside on the throne of our lives, His Holy Spirit will also guide us in being faithful to Him. But if we choose to overrule that guidance and go our own way, we will slip into carnality.

Jesus reserved some of His harshest words for Chris-

tians who lack faithfulness. He said to the church at
Laodicea:

> I know you well—you are neither hot nor cold; I
> wish you were one or the other! But since you are mere-
> ly lukewarm, I will spit you out of my mouth!
>
> You say, "I am rich, with everything I want; I don't
> need a thing!" And you don't realize that spiritually you
> are wretched and miserable and poor and blind and
> naked (Revelation 3:17).

I am afraid that we Christians may be in danger today
of our Lord pronouncing the same judgment on us. Many
of us have "left our first love"—our faithfulness to our Lord
Jesus Christ—and are paying only lip service to Christianity. No longer is Jesus Christ the most important thing
in our lives; rather, we try to carry Him around in our bag
of possessions to haul out once a week at church or on an
"as needed" basis.

We cannot possibly honor our Lord with lukewarm
faith. Neither can we be lukewarm for Christ and be joyful
and fulfilled as individuals. Our personal joy and fulfillment are directly proportionate to our faithfulness to Him
and to obeying His commandments. The Holy Spirit gives
us the power and pleasure of faithfulness as we yield to His
guidance.

---

*CHECKPOINT: Has my faithfulness to my spouse and
friends been genuine? Am I 100-percent committed to
serving my Lord?* If my honest answer is "yes," the
Holy Spirit is filling me with the pleasure of faithfulness. But if my honest answer is "no," I need to breathe
spiritually and make restitution where necessary.
Then, with the Holy Spirit's guidance, I will change my
priorities in order to truly give God first place in my
daily life.

Gentleness

Gentleness is humility born of strength and confidence. It is the quiet, moving power of the understatement. It is what enabled our Lord to act as though He were thinking, *I am strong enough to be overbearing, and I am strong enough to be gentle. I choose to be gentle.*

His gentleness changed the world.

There can be tremendous power in gentleness. Years ago, as a young businessman, I had the opportunity to talk briefly with J. C. Penney, the department store mogul who commanded thousands of employees and millions of dollars across the country. As we visited, I was impressed that Penney was one of the most gentle and humble men I had ever met.

A devoted Christian, he had built the J. C. Penney department store chain on the Golden Rule: "Do unto others as you would have them do unto you." He showed this young businessman the incredible power of gentleness in human relationships.

As I have grown older, I have realized that arrogance and boastfulness are the traits of insecure, self-important men and women. Arrogance has no place in the Christian life, for our Lord said, "Blessed are the gentle, for they shall inherit the earth" (Matthew 5:5, NAS).

He was talking about the gentleness that will become a part of us when we are filled with the Holy Spirit — the gentleness of a strong, quietly confident person who acknowledges that Jesus Christ is the source of his strength.

CHECKPOINT: *Do I lack gentleness in my life today? Do I have a tendency to boast, or be overbearing and rude?* If so, by faith I will become a gentler person by confessing my sin and appropriating God's forgiveness. I will trust God to fill me with gentleness.

Self-Control

Dwight L. Moody once said, "I have more trouble with D. L. Moody than with any other man I ever met."

His candor can make us all feel a bit better, for even the "spiritual giants" of the past and present admit that self-discipline is one of the toughest stumbling blocks along the Christian walk. Do you struggle with:

overeating?

too much TV?

smoking or drinking?

compulsive shopping and spending?

anger?

selfishness?

fear or anxiety?

a hostile or gossiping tongue?

impure thoughts?

giving in to temptation?

lack of regular time in Bible study?

lack of regular time talking with God?

sharing Christ with others?

lack of concentration on your work?

Low self-discipline in any of these areas robs us of the joy of life. In practical terms, it results in personal misery and misspent potential, and it presents a negative, repulsive witness to nonbelievers who may be watching us to gauge the validity of our faith in Christ.

We can be sure that it grieves the Holy Spirit to see us misuse the strength and power He provides to live the disciplined life. This is what led Paul to write to the Romans:

And so, dear brothers, I plead with you to give your bodies to God. Let them be a living sacrifice, holy—the kind He can accept. When you think of what He has done for you, is this too much to ask?

Don't copy the behavior and customs of this world, but be a new and different person with a fresh newness in all you do and think. Then you will learn from your own experience how His ways will really satisfy you (Romans 12:1,2).

God wants to help you live a self-controlled life, both for His glory and for your personal fulfillment. But it is only by being filled with the Spirit that you will have the supernatural self-discipline to do so.

CHECKPOINT: Am I exercising self-control in every area of life? Are my eating and spending habits pleasing to God? My thought life? My devotional life? If I answered "no" to any portion of this checkpoint, I need to yield myself totally to God through Spiritual Breathing, then keep short accounts with God as His Holy Spirit reveals sin in my life. I will trust Him to help me improve day by day.

Hand in Hand

The secret to victorious living lies not in keeping a long litany of rules and regulations, but rather in walking hand in hand with the Holy Spirit of God. As you come to know and love God, your obedience to Him will be motivated by liberty rather than by legalism. You will genuinely *desire* to live as He wants you to. He will fill you with the attributes of Christlikeness — rich pleasures indeed.

FOR REFLECTION, DISCUSSION AND ACTION

1. Jesus said, "I came that they might have life, and might have it abundantly." What does "abundant life" mean to you? Are you experiencing it? Why or why not?

2. Have you ever known a Christian who lived by the doctrine of legalism? Was that person truly happy? Why or why not?

3. Which of the fruit of the Spirit have you seen recently in members of your family, or among your friends or study group? Describe the circumstances, then take a moment to compliment and thank the individual(s) for modeling these attributes.

4. Which of the fruit of the Spirit have been weak spots in your own life? Why do you suppose they have been weak spots? What steps do you intend to take to encourage the growth of these fruits?

5. Memorize and meditate upon Galatians 5:18 (NAS): "The fruit of the Spirit is love, joy, peace, patience, kindness, goodness, faithfulness, gentleness, and self-control." Each morning, as you commit your day to Jesus Christ, ask Him to make these pleasures genuine and evident in your life.

*How Spirit-controlled living
makes a difference.*

8

Walking Through "Real Life"

*If we are living now by the Holy Spirit's power,
let us follow the Holy Spirit's leading in every part of
our lives.*

The Apostle Paul
Galatians 5:25

D r. Bright, may I speak with you alone?"
I had noticed her on the fringe of the handful of conferees who had gathered around me to ask questions following my lecture on the ministry of the Holy Spirit. And every time I glanced at her, she had looked away.

Finally the group around me thinned out. She inched forward, clutching her Bible and notebook closely, and timidly asked to speak with me. We found seats in the corner of the auditorium.

Her name was Sharon. As she struggled to begin, her eyes betrayed the fear and insecurity that were churning inside.

"I'm sorry . . . I'm nervous," she blurted.

After some halting conversation, it became evident that Sharon felt terribly insignificant. Her mother had told her more than once that she would never amount to much. She felt generally rejected whenever she tried to form close friendships. She regarded herself as homely and over-weight. She was a Christian, but the pleasure of *joy* was nonexistent in her life.

Yet, in talking with this young woman, I sensed that she was really smart and talented, with a lot to offer. Sharon was struggling with low self-esteem, and in the course of believing all the destructive thoughts about herself she was neutralizing the good things that were just waiting to surface.

I took out a sheet of paper and began drawing the Flesh vs. Spirit diagram which I shared with you in Chapter 2:

FREEDOM OF CHOICE

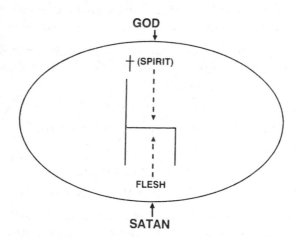

I briefly reviewed how God's Word teaches that Christians have two natures, the Flesh and the Spirit, battling for the control center of our lives.

"Sharon, when thoughts come to you saying that you're insignificant, are those thoughts coming from the Flesh or from the Spirit?" I asked.

She hesitated a moment. "From the Flesh?" she responded tentatively.

"And where do thoughts from the Flesh originate?"

"From Satan," she replied, her eyes fixed on the diagram.

"Why don't you think they originate from God?" I asked.

Sharon glanced at the top of the diagram, which illustrates how thoughts from God come to us through the Holy Spirit. "Because God wouldn't say those things about me?" she ventured.

"That's right," I said. "You are a valuable, precious person in God's sight. His message to you is that *You are significant — you are fearfully and wonderfully made.* So, to make sure we understand: If you are experiencing negative thoughts about yourself, to whom are you listening?"

Her eyes began to brighten as the realization came. "I'm listening to Satan. I'm letting my fleshly nature convince me that I'm a nobody."

"And if you listen to God, what will He tell you?"

"He will tell me that I'm precious to Him."

"And how does God speak to you?"

"Through His Holy Spirit within me."

"Which voice would you rather listen to?"

The answer was obvious. Sharon realized how destructive it can be to continue listening to disparaging thoughts about herself, because such thoughts originate with the one who wants only to neutralize her joy and effectiveness. She had allowed her thoughts to dwell on the enemy's messages instead of on God's.

I took the sheet of paper and drew a simple "radio dial" to illustrate the importance of consciously deciding which kingdom we will listen to:

MAKING THE RIGHT CHOICE

I suggested that when the self-degrading thoughts come, Sharon make a conscious decision to "turn the dial" to a better program—God's program! For the first time, a smile brightened her face and her eyes sparkled. Sharon took the sheet of paper from me and affirmed, "I'm going to picture this diagram in my mind and actually say, 'I refuse to listen to programming from Satan's kingdom— I'm turning the dial now!' "

We prayed together that the Holy Spirit would bring this concept to Sharon's mind whenever she experienced feelings of low self-esteem. She had a lifetime of self-doubt to overcome, but this simple diagram gave her a tool that gradually helped her win the battles. During the next several months, Sharon began to blossom from a timid wallflower into a beautiful rose. The fear in her eyes gradually changed to a quiet confidence. Her new smile told the world that indeed she was precious in God's sight.

Heading Off Temptation

Dave, a Christian business executive in his early forties, was alone in a hotel room. He had been away from his wife and kids for six days—and he braced himself for another long and lonely evening.

But inside his mind, thoughts were igniting. In the hotel lobby, he had noticed a particularly beautiful woman who was dressed to kill, leaving arm-in-arm with a lucky gentleman for a night on the town. Then, as he browsed the hotel newsstand, his eyes had been stopped by the sight of scantily-clad models on the covers of several men's magazines. And now Dave was in his room, with a heady maelstrom of loneliness and excitement and weakness churning inside him. As he studied the listing of the closed-circuit movies which he could order up on his TV screen, he noticed that the listing included two X-rated movies.

No one would know . . . and, after all, Dave *had* been away from his wife for six days. But then a thought came to him. A picture, in his mind, of a simple little diagram which he had learned in a class at his church.

It was the same Flesh vs. Spirit diagram I had taught to Sharon. Dave pictured in his mind the throne of his life, with input coming from both the Flesh and the Spirit.

He tells what happened next. "Immediately the thought came to me: *To whom am I listening?* And when I was honest with myself, there was no way I could say I was listening to God. I was listening to Satan, who was mounting an all-out attack on my fleshly nature.

"That thought—*To whom am I listening?*—was

enough to stop me in my tracks. I sincerely want to live for God, in private as well as in public. And when I realized that I was ignoring His voice and listening to the enemy's input, I knew I had to stop right there and 'turn the dial,' because I don't want to contaminate my mind with images that will stay with me for years to come.

"I thanked God that, through His Holy Spirit, He had brought that diagram to mind. 'I'm turning the dial now, Lord,' I prayed. 'I choose to listen to *Your* thoughts. I give *You* control of the throne of my life.' Then I pulled my Bible from my briefcase and spent two hours reading and rereading Romans 6-8."

After reading God's Word and watching a special Thursday night football game on TV, Dave slept like a baby—filled with that rich inner peace we all can experience when we stop sin in its tracks and keep Christ on the throne of our lives.

Dealing With a Bad Attitude

For almost two weeks, without realizing it, Diane had fumed with critical thoughts toward her employer. *He doesn't know what he's doing,* she would mutter to herself. *And he keeps dumping more work on me. I don't get paid enough for this!*

It didn't take long for her thoughts to translate into decreased productivity on the job. As she sat at her desk, Diane wished she were someplace else. She responded curtly to her co-workers, throwing in snide remarks about the management and the pay.

"It wasn't until a close friend asked me what was wrong that I stopped to think about my attitude," Diane says. "It had started when my bosses made a decision I didn't agree with. Instead of submitting to their leadership, I took their decision as a personal affront. I fretted and sputtered for days. I knew inside that this was not the way the Lord wanted me to act, but when you let yourself wallow in self-pity, it's like quicksand—it sucks you under before you know what's happening.

"When I realized what I had been doing, I apologized to my friend, confessed to her that my attitude had been wrong, and asked her forgiveness. Then, as soon as I was alone, I took care of things with God."

Diane had read one of my books in which I describe the process of Spiritual Breathing. In her mind she envisioned Flesh on the throne, and acknowledged that this had resulted in misery and bitterness:

THE WRONG CHOICE

GOD (Has possession of us, but we are not yielded to His control)

FLESH (Directed by Satan)

(SPIRIT)

(Still within us, but not on the throne; seeks to influence us toward God's ways)

SATAN
(Seeks control of us through the Flesh)

"First I 'exhaled'—I agreed with the Lord that my bitter attitude was sin and that I truly wanted to change," Diane says. "Then I 'inhaled'—I trusted Him to forgive, cleanse and fill me. I still felt badly that I had allowed myself to think and behave this way for so many days. And I had to apologize to several other people who had been affected by my critical spirit. But Christ was back on the throne of my life where He belongs . . ."

THE RIGHT CHOICE

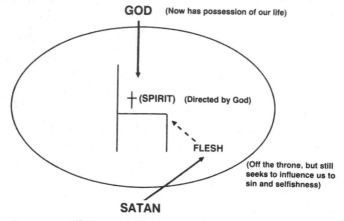

GOD (Now has possession of our life)

+ (SPIRIT) (Directed by God)

FLESH

(Off the throne, but still seeks to influence us to sin and selfishness)

SATAN

(Seeks to control us through the Flesh)

". . . and I was rejoicing in His presence again. And you know what? For some strange reason my productivity regained its edge—and my respect for my employer went up! It seems that once I listened to what the Holy Spirit was saying to me, the problem I had thought was so major took on a more realistic perspective."

I believe with all my heart that it is virtually impossible for a Spirit-filled Christian to also be miserable, for when we yield to the Holy Spirit's control He manifests supernatural joy within—joy that can transcend our circumstances and head off spiritual defeat.

Conversely, it is impossible for a bitter, depressed person to also be Spirit-filled, for the absence of joy and peace in one's life indicates that the wrong person is on the throne. Diane learned that bitterness and Spirit-filled living are mutually exclusive, and when she realized what an unhappy climate her choice had created she took the steps to be filled again with the Holy Spirit.

Overcoming Anger

"You stupid jerk!" Tony exploded, as he blasted his car horn at the driver who had just pulled out in front of him.

Within just a few moments, Tony was shaking his head in disbelief—not at the discourtesy shown by the other driver, but at how suddenly he had lost his temper. (He was also hoping the other driver had not noticed his "Jesus On Board" bumper sticker.)

"The distress I felt was the Holy Spirit saying, *Hold it, Tony. You didn't exactly bring honor to Me back there, did you? You flunked the 'self-control' checkpoint.*"

As Tony continued driving, he confessed his angry outburst, then thanked God for His promise to forgive and cleanse him of the sin. It had been momentary, but it had been ugly . . . and making things right with God was just as important in this "little sin" as it is in a "big sin."

And Tony has learned from the experience. "It startled me to see the anger that is part of my fleshly nature. So I've been asking God to keep me from exploding like that—and to help me not to even *think* those angry thoughts.

"And He *is* helping me. In my neighborhood, for example, we have laws about loose dogs. But one particular neighbor has no reservations about letting his monstrous dog run loose to leave monstrous deposits on my lawn. My natural reaction would be to scoop up that deposit with a shovel and fling it onto my neighbor's porch. But I can sense the Holy Spirit telling me, *Smile. Relax. It really isn't that important, is it?*

"That's the Holy Spirit in action—in the nitty-gritty parts of life! He helps me keep short accounts with God, and He is helping me respond with the fruit of the Spirit even when people do something I consider rude."

"To Whom Am I Listening?"

Like Sharon, Dave, Diane and Tony, you can benefit from the power of the Holy Spirit in the down-to-earth challenges that life brings your way. The two concepts which we reviewed in this chapter, the Flesh vs. Spirit diagram and Spiritual Breathing, will prove invaluable to you as you take the Spirit-filled walk through real life.

As you saw with Dave, the Flesh vs. Spirit concept can actually help serve as a *preventive* to straying off course. When Dave was struggling with temptation in his hotel room, the Holy Spirit prompted him to stop and ask himself: *To whom am I listening?*

Let me encourage you to employ this same strategy in your own daily walk. Make a commitment today that, whenever you are in a tempting situation, you will ask that question: *To whom am I listening?* The answer will be quick and clear, for the Holy Spirit's conviction is already underway. When He reveals that you are listening to the messages of the Flesh, consciously "turn the dial" and listen to God's program.

While this simple diagram can help you in the prevention of sin, it also has helped hundreds of Christians recognize the Holy Spirit's *conviction of an ongoing weakness or sin.* Sharon saw that her negative self-image was the result of listening to Satan's lies rather than God's love. Diane, after nearly two weeks of anger and bitterness, finally realized she had been listening to the wrong messages from the wrong source. Both women decided to "turn the dial" and tune in to God's truth.

Exhale, Inhale

The second concept, Spiritual Breathing, helped Sharon, Diane and Tony confess their sin and restore fellowship with God. As they pictured Christ reclaiming the throne at their invitation, they knew by faith that God was keeping His promises to forgive and cleanse them of their unrighteousness, and to fill them afresh with His Holy Spirit.

Again, I strongly encourage you to utilize the principle of Spiritual Breathing as you walk through real life. Commit today that you will deal with sin as soon as the Holy Spirit convicts you. Then, learn from your experience—acknowledge your natural weaknesses and ask God to strengthen you to pass the next test. He will . . . and you can!

To Spend or Not to Spend?

Jeff and Anne tell how both of these concepts helped them turn their personal finances around. On a fall day they were window shopping at the mall when an alluring display of ski gear caught their attention.

"We enjoy skiing, and our equipment was several years old," says Anne. "So when we saw the display, especially with a *SALE* sign propped up against the ski boots, we felt we *had* to check it out."

"Skis, boots, bindings and ski poles for both of us, even on sale, would have cost almost $1500," Jeff recalls. "All the usual thoughts went through our minds, like *We really do need to treat ourselves once in a while. We can't ski as well with out-of-style gear. We can put it on Visa.*"

But Jeff and Anne had an underlying problem: They were already deeply in debt. Instead of "treating themselves once in a while," they had made a habit of it. One "special sale" after another had turned their cash flow to chaos. Their consumer debt (debts in addition to their mortgage) now totalled almost 30 percent of their income—a sure sign of trouble. Each month, on five different credit cards, they could barely meet the minimum payments, let alone pay down the principal.

Anne continues the story: "Jeff and I had allowed a desire for things and immediate gratification to invade our value system. As a result, our finances were a mess. We had quit giving to our church, we had no savings program, we even argued over grocery money. Any discretionary income was going toward making all those minimum payments on the credit cards."

"I think we knew that we weren't glorifying God in the way we handled our money," Jeff adds. "But we had never really talked about it or done anything about it— until that day at the mall."

"We were *this* close to putting that ski gear on our Visa card," says Anne, holding two fingers close together. "As Jeff was getting the card out of his wallet, I could tell he was struggling. I touched his arm and said, 'Are you thinking what I'm thinking?' And he smiled at me, put the card back in his wallet, and answered, 'I don't know. Let's go talk.' "

Jeff and Anne left the sporting goods store and sat down on a bench to think and talk.

Several weeks earlier, they had heard a friend describe my Flesh vs. Spirit diagram, and now Jeff couldn't take his mind off that concept. "The thought kept going through my mind: *To whom are we listening?* I had felt a mounting unrest inside me as I had prepared to make this new purchase. And after learning this concept, I'm convinced it was the Holy Spirit who brought that question to mind.

"We were already in financial difficulty because of our

materialism and lack of self-control. And as Anne and I sat
on that bench, we admitted that we were again listening to
the desires of the Flesh. We had no business considering
such a purchase. We needed to deal with the underlying
problem inside of us and then clean up our financial situation."

Anne remembers how she and Jeff agreed that they
needed to "turn the dial" and listen to what God was saying
about wise financial management. Then they prayed
together, their eyes open as they sat in the middle of that
busy mall, confessing to God their poor stewardship and
materialism. As they appropriated God's forgiveness and
the filling of His Holy Spirit, they asked God to give them
the discipline to say "no" to temptation, to get their debts
paid, and to renew their financial giving to their church.

"And the Holy Spirit is helping us," testifies Anne.
"We're now painfully aware of our fleshly tendencies in this
area. If Christ is on the throne of our lives, whenever we
are tempted to spend frivolously He reminds us of our commitment. We're praying together about each decision that
comes along, and He is giving us the self-control to say, 'No
thanks.' "

"We still want to get new ski gear some day," Jeff has-
tens to add. "Only this time, we're saving up in advance.
No more heavy debt for us. But you know, our skiing hasn't
suffered one bit. We've enjoyed some great family ski days
on our old equipment. In fact, if we had bought the new ski
gear, we probably couldn't have afforded to go!"

Restoring a Union

Paul and Jennifer were ready to give up on their marriage. After eleven years and three children, their union
had become lifeless and fragile.

The romance which had fueled the early years was

gone. Communication had disintegrated from meaningful dialogues to shallow, utilitarian exchanges. Personal idiosyncracies which initially had brought laughter now proved irritating.

Both Paul and Jennifer were Christians, but for some time they had been living in defeat. At church on Sunday morning they were usually able to come across as a happy Christian couple. But as soon as they got home they would turn the TV on and the happiness off.

Arguments broke out over the smallest things. And the aftershocks would linger for days.

Why not get a divorce? Jennifer said to herself more than once. *Life has to be better than this. I'm missing out.*

It's sure not like it used to be, Paul thought as he vegetated in front of the TV. *She bugs me and I bug her. Maybe we both should start over . . . but I sure can't afford separate alimony and child support . . .*

But divorce would be so embarrassing, Jennifer argued in frustration. *Our family, our friends at church — and the children. How would we explain it to them?*

And so their dismal lives continued to go downhill, until Jennifer attended a home Bible study on the importance of being filled with the Holy Spirit.

She quickly recognized that she and Paul were what the Bible calls "carnal" people (1 Corinthians 3:1-3). She and Paul had allowed their selfish natures to take control of the throne of their lives, and as a result they were getting their messages from the selfish Flesh and not from the loving Spirit.

Can this be it? Jennifer wondered as the study leader concluded the lesson. *Can this be why things have been falling apart?*

Later that night, Jennifer did what the study leader

had suggested: She asked God to reveal any unconfessed sin in her life. As the Holy Spirit brought specific sins to mind, she confessed them and trusted God to forgive and cleanse her. "Lord Jesus," she concluded, "I give you control of the throne of my life. Help me to be a good wife to Paul. Help us to live as You want us to live."

The next day, she told Paul what had happened. He was noncommittal at first, but within a week Paul also realized the need to be filled with the Spirit.

"We both made things right with God and with each other," he says, "and we 'turned the dial' to be sure we weren't listening to the messages of the Flesh any longer. We had some negative habits to work through, but we know now that when we let the Holy Spirit do His job, our marriage will work."

Gradually, Paul and Jennifer's romance has been rekindled. Their communication patterns have become more constructive and uplifting. They are praying together regularly, and they try to gauge their attitudes and conduct by the standards in God's Word. By keeping the Holy Spirit on the throne, they are tapped in to His supply of supernatural *agape* love and are able to be genuinely interested in what is best for each other.

God indeed cares about real life. Don't ever let anyone tell you that your problem is too large, too small or too mundane for Him. He is helping Jeff and Anne restore their financial integrity. He is helping Paul and Jennifer rebuild their marriage—all through the power of His Holy Spirit.

Harness the Secret

To whom are *you* listening? Whenever you face temptation, discouragement, inner turmoil, conflict with another person, or any situation which might rob you of the joy of the Master, please . . . ask yourself that question.

Then answer it honestly. Acknowledge that you have been listening to the enemy of your soul, the one who wants to make you a miserable, fruitless individual.

Consciously "turn the dial" to listen to God, the One who loves you so much that He sacrificed His only Son for you. His counsel is wise, it is right, and it is *always* in your best interest.

Experience the joy of "walking in the Spirit" by keeping Him on the throne. Keep those accounts short by breathing spiritually the moment the Holy Spirit tells you something is wrong.

Do so, and you will have harnessed the secret. Your life will never be the same.

FOR REFLECTION, DISCUSSION AND ACTION

1. Of the six stories in this chapter, which situation did you identify with the most? Why? Describe the circumstances and how you responded.

2. What did you learn or review in this chapter that will be of significant help to you the next time you encounter that type of situation?

3. Suppose a Christian friend comes to you and says, "I'm really struggling with temptation . . . What do I do?" What (besides "I'll pray for you") would you say to help him?

4. Share a recent incident from your life in which Spiritual Breathing helped you keep short accounts with God.

5. Commit today to asking the question, *To whom am I listening?* whenever you wrestle with temptation or negative or cynical thoughts.

Do not allow what you don't know about the Holy Spirit to keep you from embracing what you do know.

9

Questions People Ask About the Holy Spirit

My prayer for all of them is that they will be of one heart and mind.

Jesus Christ
John 17:21

The auditorium was packed. More than four thousand men and women from the Seattle, Washington, area had come together for training at one of our Lay Institutes for Evangelism, and I had just finished my message on how to be filled with the Holy Spirit.

A gentleman in his early sixties, smiling ear to ear, approached me with his hand extended.

"Dr. Bright, I've just retired from twenty years of missionary work in Africa," Len told me as we shook hands. "Today, as you spoke, I settled accounts with God and was filled with the Spirit. For twenty years I have tried to serve

God on the mission field, but I have little results to show
for it. I realize now that I was serving Him in the energy of
the Flesh."

Len's eyes sparkled as he continued. "I was like the
disciples before Pentecost—relying on my own abilities instead of God's power. I was often frustrated and discouraged.

"This message is something every Christian worker
needs to hear! I want to return to the mission field to help
spread it to the other missionaries—I know many of them
are still searching for what I sought all these years and discovered only today.

"I want to teach them what you taught me, so they can
minister more effectively and teach others how they, too,
can be filled with the Holy Spirit."

Len is typical of so many Christians who want to serve
our Lord, but fail to tap into the source of power that will
make their service fruitful and rewarding. Because he
didn't understand the ministry of the Holy Spirit, he chose
to ignore the role the Spirit wanted to fulfill in his life. The
results: spiritual defeat and an ineffective ministry.

Sandra is another who inadvertently let her joy be
neutralized by what she didn't understand. A Christian for
four years, she had benefited from our initial training on
the Spirit-filled life. But then she became confused, for a
Christian acquaintance at work had told her that unless
she exhibited a certain "spiritual gift," she had not received
the "baptism of the Holy Spirit" and therefore was not
Spirit-filled.

"I went into a tailspin," Sandra remembers. "My
friend meant well, but I was devastated. I struggled for
several months afterward, wondering if there was some
mystical experience I had missed—and if so, why. I even
began to doubt whether I was truly a Christian."

Len and Sandra demonstrate the importance of addressing some of the questions people often ask about the Holy Spirit. You may have heard these questions, or even asked them, yourself. Some have clear answers, while others seem to fall into that category of divine mystery which God has chosen not to fully explain to us.

Before we look at a few of the more common questions, it might be beneficial at this point for you to review Chapters 3 and 4 to overview the essential basics about who the Holy Spirit is and what He does in the life of the believer. Many of the typical questions people raise are answered in those chapters.

Here, then, are some of the other questions which frequently come up.

"Why all this talk about the Holy Spirit? Let's talk about Jesus Christ."

A minister friend once said this to me, and I have heard the same sentiment from others as well.

It is true that our purpose is to exalt and glorify Jesus Christ, and it is important that we never lose sight of that. But we must keep in mind that it is impossible for us to exalt and glorify the Lord in our fleshly power. We need the Holy Spirit in order to live a life that brings honor to Christ.

Jesus Himself said that the Holy Spirit would be the key to honoring Him. "But when the Holy Spirit has come upon you, you will receive power to testify about me with great effect," He told the disciples in Acts 1:8. Earlier, He said that "He [the Holy Spirit] shall praise me and bring me great honor by showing you my glory" (John 16:14).

It is also impossible to know Jesus Christ as Savior and Lord apart from the inner working of the Holy Spirit. When Nicodemus asked Jesus how to be born again, our Lord replied, "Unless one is born of water and the Spirit, he cannot enter the kingdom of God" (John 3:5).

The Holy Spirit enables us to become Christians, understand God's Word, live holy lives, pray, and witness effectively. Without Him, we are rendered useless in our service of the Lord Jesus Christ.

So while it is a mistake to focus entirely on the Holy Spirit, as some groups tend to do, it is also a mistake to ignore the Holy Spirit. Since He is the key to supernatural living, we will benefit the work of Christ only if we appropriate His power by faith and show others how to do the same.

*"Some people I know are emotional about their faith.
I get stirred up once in awhile, but I just don't feel
excited all the time like these people do.
Is something wrong with me?"*

When you received Christ, you may or may not have had an emotional experience. Feelings are not what save us; God's Word says we are saved *through faith* (Ephesians 2:8).

God also instructs us to live each day in the same way: "As you therefore have received Christ Jesus the Lord, so walk in Him" (Colossians 2:6, NAS). On some occasions, such as a particularly joyful or convicting or heartbreaking situation, we may become emotional. But for the most part, we may not feel deeply ecstatic or emotional.

Many Christians have understood this point better after reviewing a simple drawing I use to show how we should not depend on our feelings:

The engine (FACT) signifies that the promise of God's Word—not our feelings—is our authority and guide for the Christian life. We are to live by FAITH in the trustworthiness of God Himself and His Word. Our FEELINGS (emotions) should be the *result* of our faith, not a *cause* of our faith.

The train will run with or without the caboose. However, it would be useless to try to pull the train by the caboose. In the same way we, as Christians, are not to depend on feelings or emotions—we must place our trust in the trustworthiness of God and His promises. Feelings will vary, but the *fact* of God's trustworthiness remains constant.

We should not fear our emotions—God created them for our benefit. But at the same time, it grieves the Holy Spirit if we *seek* emotional experiences, for these can distract us from the work He truly wants to do in us. I encourage you to be cautious if you feel the need for some type of experience in order to affirm that you are yielded to the Holy Spirit.

In an earlier book, *The Holy Spirit: The Key to Supernatural Living,* I shared some important thoughts about the psyche of Christians who seek emotionalism. These thoughts bear repeating:

> People who attend emotionally charged meetings often reach the point where they need something more dramatic and even ecstatic to satisfy them. In the process, some become hardened and even resort to manufacturing counterfeit experiences. Others have indicated that they have become hypocritical in trying to keep up with those who share dramatic personal experiences.
>
> We are told by medical specialists that, as one becomes addicted to a drug, his body develops a tolerance to that drug and his craving increases. When this hap-

> pens, the user must increase the dosage or switch to a
> more powerful drug.
>
>   It is the same with emotional experiences that are
> of the Flesh and not of the Spirit. An "experience addict"
> encounters frustration and a growing lack of fulfillment.
> He must therefore satisfy his craving through stronger
> and stronger emotional experiences.[1]

This is why God's Word emphasizes that we are to
walk by faith, not by emotion. Our loving Lord wants us to
focus on Himself and His Word. The successful Christian
life is one of calm inner trust in God, made manifest not in
emotionalism but in love, joy, peace, patience, kindness,
goodness, faithfulness, gentleness and self-control.

> *"Some friends of mine put a lot of emphasis*
> *on 'spiritual gifts.' What are these gifts*
> *and what do they mean to me?"*

One of the apostle Paul's chief messages was that
Christians need each other; we are to love, help, encourage
and pray for one another in our efforts to advance the cause
of Jesus Christ. To do so, Paul taught, the Holy Spirit has
given each of us one or more special abilities called
"spiritual gifts."

Each Christian receives at least one gift from the Holy
Spirit: "God gives us many kinds of special abilities . . . the
Holy Spirit displays God's power through each of us as a
means of helping the entire church" (1 Corinthians 12:4,7).

In three separate New Testament letters, Paul compiled lists of these gifts. (For definitions of the spiritual gifts
mentioned in these passages, see Appendix C, "Spiritual
Gifts Defined.")

    1 Corinthians 12:   wisdom
                           knowledge
                           faith

1 Corinthians 12: healing
                  miracles
                  prophecy
                  discerning of spirits
                  tongues
                  interpretation of tongues
                  apostleship
                  teaching
                  helping
                  administration

Romans 12: leadership
                  exhortation
                  giving
                  mercy

Ephesians 4: apostle
                  prophet
                  evangelist
                  pastor-teacher

It is important to note that every spiritual gift is oriented toward the benefit of others and the glory of God. Not one is intended for use by a self-centered Christian whose main interests lie in personal gain (as illustrated by the story of Simon in Acts 8:14-24). We need each other, and God wants us to work together unselfishly to build each other up and spread His Word.

Paul underscored this point in Ephesians 4:12,13:

> Why is it that He gives us these special abilities to do certain things best? It is that God's people will be equipped to do better work for Him, building up the Church, the body of Christ, to a position of strength and maturity; until finally we all believe alike about our salvation and about our Savior, God's Son, and all become full-grown in the Lord—yes, to the point of being filled full of Christ.

Read that again—it's important! Clearly, we have an obligation to use our spiritual gifts to help equip others for effective Christian service, to help build up the church, and to strengthen one another in Christian maturity.

Take a quick look around Tom's living room, where he is leading a home Bible study. Tom has special interests and abilities in teaching, and he is exercising this gift by helping others learn and apply God's Word.

To his left is Dorian, who feels a strong burden for anyone who experiences trauma or sorrow. Her gift of mercy prompts her to be quick with an encouraging word or a helping hand.

Next is Joe, who has a noticeable ability to organize key events and make sure everything comes off without too many hitches. Joe's gift is probably that of administration, and he is using it to head up the group's evangelistic and social events during the coming year.

Dennis is an encourager. His enthusiasm is contagious, and on many occasions Dennis has helped the others set aside their fatigue or discouragement and praise the Lord in spite of their circumstances. When Dennis uses his gift of exhortation, others get their eyes off themselves and back on Christ.

Georgia is always the first to offer assistance. She loves helping others. Frequently, she calls Tom and offers to photocopy the study questions or bring the flip chart from the church so he can be free to study and prepare. Her gift of helping provides an essential service to the group.

From this small-group example, it is easy to see that when any group of believers uses their spiritual gifts unselfishly, for the glory of God, the Holy Spirit can draw people close together and accomplish great things through them.

*"Do certain gifts make some individuals more
important to the body of Christ than others?"*

No. Paul demonstrated how each member of the
church is just as important as the other when he compared
the church to the physical body of Christ:

> The body has many parts, not just one part. If the
> foot says, "I am not a part of the body because I am not
> a hand," that does not make it any less a part of the body.
> And what would you think if you heard an ear say, "I am
> only an ear, and not an eye"? Would that make it any less
> a part of the body?
>
> Suppose the whole body were an eye — then how
> would you hear? Or if your whole body were just one big
> ear, how could you smell anything?
>
> But that isn't the way God has made us. He has
> made many parts for our bodies and has put each part
> just where He wants it. What a strange thing a body
> would be if it had only one part! So He has made many
> parts, but still there is only one body.
>
> The eye can never say to the hand, "I don't need
> you." The head can't say to the feet, "I don't need you"
> (1 Corinthians 12:14-21).

Some gifts may be more visible than others — a person
exercising the gift of teaching will probably be noticed by
many more people than the person using his gift of mercy.
But because some gifts are more visible than others, we
must be cautious not to fall into the trap of considering one
person or gift more important to the body of Christ than
another person or gift. In like manner, as Paul emphasized
in the Scripture above, a Christian should never consider
his own gift unimportant and long for another.

*"What kind of emphasis, then, should we place
on spiritual gifts in the Christian life?"*

We have seen how God's Word teaches that the use of
our spiritual gifts for God's glory is important — in fact, it
is a must.

But at the same time, we must be careful that we do
not focus so intently on the gifts that we neglect their purpose. Some individuals focus so much on "discovering their
personal gifts" that they become proud of their gift and un-
willing to serve in any way which seems unrelated to it. I
have even heard Christians say, when given an opportunity
to serve their church or help another person, "Oh, I can't
do *that* — it's not my gift!"

Preoccupation with spiritual gifts was a mistake made
by the Christians at Corinth. Paul began his letter to them
acknowledging that they had been given "every spiritual
gift and power for doing [God's] will" (1 Corinthians 1:7).
But instead of glorifying Christ or building up one another,
they were exercising their gifts to make themselves look
good. Their efforts were motivated by the Flesh, not by the
Spirit, as they emphasized their gifts so strongly that they
missed the point of it all.

Throughout this letter, and culminated by the classic
"love chapter," Paul emphasized that the use of the
spiritual gifts is worthless unless motivated by God's *agape*
love.

> If I speak with the tongues of men and of angels,
> but do not have love, I have become a noisy gong or a
> clanging cymbal. If I had the gift of prophecy and knew
> all about what is going to happen in the future . . . but
> didn't love others, what good would it do? Even if I had
> the gift of faith so that I could speak to a mountain and
> make it move, I would still be worth nothing at all
> without love (1 Corinthians 13:1-3, NAS).

In the next chapter of his letter, Paul wrote that we should "Pursue love, yet desire earnestly spiritual gifts" (1 Corinthians 14:1, NAS). Without love, our gifts and efforts are meaningless; at the same time, if we truly love others, we will use our spiritual gifts to edify them. But we must do so in a spirit of gentleness and humility.

"What is the baptism with the Holy Spirit?"

There is much disagreement over what, exactly, this term means. Some Christians believe that the "baptism with the Holy Spirit," which we find in several New Testament passages including Mark 1:8 and Acts 1:5, is actually a second experience on a separate occasion following one's conversion. Many of these Christians believe that the Holy Spirit fills the Christian at this time, usually bringing on a profound emotional release and/or the experience of speaking in tongues.

Others contend that this baptism takes place at the same time one receives Christ as Savior and Lord and that it more accurately describes an inner spiritual repositioning of the individual than an outward experience.

Early in Paul's discussion of spiritual gifts, he pictured each of us as vital parts of a body in order to encourage us to use our gifts unselfishly and not to long for another person's ability. He then carried the metaphor further by showing that we are all essential parts of *Christ's "body"* — our fellow Christians at church, across the country and around the world:

> Our bodies have many parts, but the many parts make up only one body when they are all put together. So it is with the "body" of Christ. Each of us is a part of the one body of Christ . . . but the Holy Spirit has fitted us all together into one body. *We have been baptized into Christ's body by the one Spirit, and have all been given that same Holy Spirit* (1 Corinthians 12:12,13).

In Galatians, Paul compared our new life in Christ to taking on a sparkling new wardrobe:

> For all of you who were baptized into Christ have clothed yourselves in Christ (Galatians 3:27).

The physical act of water baptism is a public testimony on our part that we have discarded the old life and taken on a new life in Jesus Christ. Paul used this act as a fitting analogy of what the Holy Spirit did inside us when we received Christ. From 1 Corinthians we can see that when the Holy Spirit baptized us He removed us from the "body" of Satan and made us a vital part of the "body" of Christ. In Galatians, Paul taught that the Holy Spirit discarded and buried our sinful value system and clothed us with the righteous value system of Jesus Christ.

That is what the Holy Spirit's baptism accomplishes inside of us. He buries the old life and establishes us in the new life. We are baptized into the family of God when we receive Christ as Savior and Lord, and at the same time we are "sealed in Him" according to Ephesians 1:13 and 4:30. (To avoid confusion, remember that this is not the physical act of water baptism. That comes later, as a public acknowledgment of what has already taken place inside us.)

It is important to emphasize that our salvation does not depend on which view we hold regarding the baptism of the Holy Spirit; nor should our unity and effectiveness as believers be neutralized by our differing viewpoints. Most Christians do agree that the baptism takes place, for such is clearly stated in the above Scriptures. Our disagreements over the timing and means, however, should not keep us from loving one another and working together toward the common goal of introducing the world to Christ.

"Is it necessary that I speak in tongues to know that I am saved and filled with the Holy Spirit?"

This is the question that had Sandra doubting her own salvation, and unfortunately it has caused much confusion among Christians around the world.

In fact, the gift of tongues (speaking to God or to others in unlearned languages or utterances) has proven to be one of the most divisive issues of the Christian faith in our time. Over the years my heart has been broken again and again as I have seen churches and entire ministries split apart because of disagreements over the practice of speaking in tongues.

Some Background: Tongues in the Early Church

The gift of tongues was originally given to the apostles at Pentecost (see Acts 2) as a sign to the Jews living in Jerusalem. These Jews were "devout men, from every nation under heaven" (2:5), who apparently had retained their native languages. As the apostles were filled with the Holy Spirit, God gave them the supernatural ability to speak to these Jews in their own dialects.

This got the Jews' attention! The New American Standard version reports:

> And they were amazed and marveled, saying, "Why, are not all these who are speaking Galileans? And how is it that we each hear them in our own language to which we were born?" (Acts 2:7,8)

Peter, empowered with the Spirit of God, saw the amazement of the Jews and spoke passionately of how Jesus Christ had fulfilled the cherished prophecy of the Messiah. When Peter finished speaking, *three thousand men and women* received Christ as Savior and Lord!

The gift of foreign languages had been a sign from God to the Jews as well as a practical tool for communicating the gospel to a diverse audience.

The gift of tongues is mentioned elsewhere in Acts. In Chapter 10 Peter was speaking to another gathering:

> And while Peter was still speaking these words, the Holy Spirit fell upon all those who were listening to the message.
>
> And all the circumcised believers who had come with Peter were amazed, because the gift of the Holy Spirit had been poured out upon the Gentiles also.
>
> For they were hearing them speaking with tongues and exalting God (Acts 10:44-46).

Another account of tongues in Acts takes place in Chapter 19, where the apostle Paul came across a group of Christian disciples who were unaware of who the Holy Spirit is.

> And when Paul had laid his hands upon them, the Holy Spirit came on them, and they began speaking with tongues and prophesying (19:6).

At least among these particular groups, the ability to speak in tongues was an indication that the Holy Spirit had entered their lives. He empowered them to speak in this way for the purpose of glorifying God and leading others to Him.

Many scholars believe the gift of tongues may have been limited strictly to speaking in actual foreign languages, which is what took place in Acts 2. Others believe that the gift of tongues eventually took on another form: ecstatic utterances not resembling any known human language. It is believed that these utterances were actually the Holy Spirit praying through the believer in a heavenly dialect or "prayer language," and that Paul differentiated these two forms as "the tongues of men and of angels" in 1 Corinthians 13.

In modern times, "the tongues of angels" has become

the predominant form among those who speak in tongues.

With this background, we come back to the question that has created such confusion today. Is it necessary to speak in tongues to know we are filled with the Holy Spirit?

One View: Tongues No Longer Valid

One school of thought generally teaches that the gift of tongues (as well as certain other gifts such as miracles and healing) was intended only for the early church, to help them ignite the spread of the gospel through the world in a variety of foreign languages. Those of this group who acknowledge the second form of tongues (ecstatic utterances) contend that it also was given only to the early church as a sign to unbelievers of the Holy Spirit's working. The gifts of miracles, healing and tongues were key aspects of the apostles' early ministry, for they helped draw thousands of nonbelievers to receive Jesus Christ. However, after the New Testament books were written and gathered together, the prominence of these gifts diminished as the gospel continued to be spread in written form. Since the original purpose for miracles, healing and tongues (the quick spread of the gospel throughout the nations) was fulfilled by the early church, many Christians believe these gifts are no longer valid. Some even contend that speaking in any form of tongues today is unscriptural and possibly satanic rather than of God.

Another View: Tongues Still Valid

The other school of thought is that while the gift of actual foreign languages may have diminished, the practice of ecstatic utterances or prayer languages continues to be the Holy Spirit's special sign of His filling.

Most who subscribe to this view look upon their first experience of tongues as the "baptism with (or in) the Holy Spirit," the sign that they have been filled. Some among this group regard speaking in tongues as the "initial evidence" that one is Spirit-filled, and believe that one has not been baptized with the Holy Spirit unless he has spoken in tongues.

Each school of thought also has those who take a more moderate, tolerant view. Among Christians who believe tongues are no longer necessary, for example, you will find those who believe that tongues may still be a valid gift for some, but not for everyone. Among Christians who believe tongues are still valid, you will find some who believe that this gift is available for everyone but that it is not necessarily the "initial evidence," and they do not regard as unspiritual those who have not experienced it.

The Crucial Point

I cannot find one Scripture which definitively says that the gift of tongues is no longer valid today. Neither can I find one which says that speaking in tongues is necessary in order to know that we are filled with the Spirit. But what *is* clear from God's Word is that it is absolutely wrong for Christians to become preoccupied or divided over this issue.

"Behold, how beautiful and pleasant it is for brethren to dwell together in unity!" the psalmist wrote (Psalm 133:1, KJV).

Our Lord's dramatic prayer in John 17 emphasized His desire for harmony among believers:

> I am not praying for these alone [His disciples] but also for the future believers who will come to me because of the testimony of these. *My prayer for all of them is that they will be of one heart and mind*, just as you and I are, Father—that just as you are in me and I am in you, so they will be in us, and the world will believe you sent me (17:20,21).

On many occasions the apostle Paul exhorted Christians not to allow disagreements to divide them. One of his most urgent pleas was to the Corinthian church:

> But, dear brothers, I beg you in the name of the
> Lord Jesus Christ to stop arguing among yourselves. Let
> there be real harmony so that there won't be splits in the
> church. I plead with you to be of one mind, united in
> thought and purpose (1 Corinthians 1:10).

In this same letter Paul included 1 Corinthians 13.
Resoundingly, he proclaimed that speaking in tongues and
all of the other spiritual gifts pale in importance next to the
primary characteristic of the Spirit-filled walk: love. Therefore, if the issue of speaking in tongues causes us to cease
loving one another, we are giving it too much importance.
Above all, we are to be unified in spite of our diversity,
motivated by love rather than the desire that everyone
agree with us.

The True Signs of Spirit-filled Living

While for some groups of early believers being filled
with the Spirit resulted in their speaking in unknown tongues, God's Word does not command that we speak in tongues. But it *does* command that we be filled with the Spirit
(Galatians 5:18).

The Bible also states clearly that the fruit (result) of
being Spirit-filled is "love, joy, peace, patience, kindness,
goodness, faithfulness, gentleness and self-control." These
are the true biblical indicators of the Spirit-filled life.

I do not speak in tongues, but I have several dear
Christian friends in other ministries who do. I know
without a shadow of doubt that these men and women are
dedicated, godly brothers and sisters in Christ who live effective, exemplary lives. So while I do not fully understand
this aspect of their Christian practice, I cannot say that
praying in tongues is not from God in this day and age. I
deeply love and respect these men and women of God, and
they love and respect me. None of us tries to pressure the

other into accepting our views. We are resolved not to allow an issue such as this to destroy the harmony our Lord prayed for in John 17: "My prayer for them is that they might be of one heart and mind."

Living in Harmony

We probably will never learn the definitive answer on tongues in this life. But let me suggest four important principles that can help us "be of one heart and mind" as our Lord wants us to be.

First, the gift of tongues must always be exercised in accordance with the biblical guidelines explained in 1 Corinthians 14. If you already speak in tongues, I strongly encourage you to study this passage thoroughly, after reading 1 Corinthians 12 and 13.

Second, those who have the gift of tongues must exercise it in love and humility, not pressuring others to speak in tongues or regarding them as unspiritual if they do not.

Third, those who do not have the gift of tongues must accept with love those who claim to have it.

Fourth, all of us must remember that speaking in tongues is only one of the spiritual gifts, not the central core of the Christian life. We must not be like the Corinthian Christians who had allowed this debate to turn them into squabbling, carnal Christians. Instead, as Paul wrote so strongly, we are to love each other and work together to glorify God by taking His message to the whole world.

FOR REFLECTION, DISCUSSION AND ACTION

1. Why do you feel it is important to have an understanding of the role of the Holy Spirit in the world and in your life?

2. A friend comes to you and says, "I've confessed all my known sins and committed myself to obeying God. But I

just don't *feel* excited!" How will you help him understand the proper place for emotions in his Christian life?

3. For what purpose(s) does God give each Christian certain "spiritual gifts"? In what ways can spiritual gifts be abused?

4. A fellow Christian comes to you and says, "Mary told me I'm not Spirit-filled if I haven't spoken in tongues." What will you say to help your friend gain the proper perspective on this issue?

5. What attitude are we to have toward fellow believers with whom we disagree? Why do you think God considers this attitude to be so important?

6. Read and reflect on Philippians 2:1-10. What would you say is the central theme of this important passage? How does it apply to you?

1. Bill Bright, *The Holy Spirit: The Key to Supernatural Living* (San Bernardino, CA: Here's Life Publishers, 1980), p. 66.

Six privileges essential to
spiritual power.

10

Delightful Disciplines of the Inner Life

To become Christlike is the only thing in the whole world worth caring for, the thing before which every ambition of man is folly and all lower achievement vain.

Henry Drummond

Sam was hungry. He had been so busy that he hadn't eaten all day. So when work was over and he pulled up to the Hungry Man Smorgasbord, he was ready for a feast.

And what a feast it was, spread out before him like a royal banquet! The chefs had prepared prime rib, baked ham, honey-roasted chicken, and several seafood delights. Sam could also enjoy lasagna, enchiladas, and sweet and sour pork. Crisp vegetables and fruit salads. Homemade soups. Sumptuous cakes, deep-dish pies and gourmet ice cream. And he could top it off with milk, coffee, tea, soft drinks, even designer mineral water.

Sam took a tray, added utensils wrapped around a linen napkin, and started down the line.

The salads looked delicious. But as he approached them his mind darted to the problem he had wrestled with at work that morning. Before he knew it he had passed the salads and was standing before the selection of meats.

But he couldn't decide which entrée he wanted . . . he thought of closing his eyes and pointing to one, but people behind him were growing restless. So he moved on. He felt so rushed that he passed right by the Italian, Mexican and Chinese foods.

He grabbed a packet of saltine crackers, but missed the soups because he was thinking about the TV series that would be on later that evening. Then he saw someone in the line who reminded him of a client at the office. That must have been when he passed by the desserts without seeing them.

By this time he had arrived at the beverage section, but was so distracted that he could barely select a glass to push against the chrome faucet for some tepid tap water.

The cashier looked at Sam curiously. "Is that all you're having?"

"It'll do," he replied. "I'm in kind of a hurry."

Sam feasted on his crackers and water, then got up to leave. *I wonder why I'm still hungry,* he thought, as he walked to his car.

And later that evening, as he stared at the TV screen, he thought, *Why do I feel so weak?* . . .

I could tell as soon as Doug and I shook hands that something was wrong.

This sharp, mid-30ish man had served diligently on

our staff for more than three years. Whenever I had seen him, his bright smile and sparkling eyes had been of encouragement to me. Today, though, Doug's smile just wasn't quite the same. As we sat at the sofa and armchair arrangement in my office, he got right to the point.

"Bill, I asked to see you because I'm struggling."

During the past several weeks, Doug told me, he had felt as though he were ministering from an empty reservoir. His passion for serving Christ had evaporated. The spiritual enthusiasm and joy that had characterized his daily life was no longer there.

"The other day I was around some happy Christians," he sighed, "and my reaction was, *They'll get over it.* I've noticed myself becoming cynical over other people's joy. I've tried confessing my negative attitude as soon as the Holy Spirit convicts me, and I consciously try to return the throne of my life to the Lord. But I'm still feeling dry—almost as if I don't care."

Doug went on to describe some other symptoms of his spiritual struggle. When he had finished, I thanked him for his honesty. "You've come to a brother in Christ for help," I affirmed him, "and that is often the toughest step.

"Doug," I continued, "as you know, I strongly believe that it is impossible for a Spirit-filled Christian to be miserable, and it's impossible for a miserable Christian to be Spirit-filled, because the fruit of the Spirit includes joy and peace. Would you agree with that?"

He pondered my question for a moment. "I know that in my head, Bill. But I'm not experiencing it in my heart. I think I'm controlled by the Holy Spirit, and I've asked God to reveal any unconfessed sin in my life so I can breathe spiritually. But I still feel weak and worthless. Something is short-circuiting the joy and power of the Holy Spirit in my life."

I could tell that it was difficult for him to admit these things to me. I again assured Doug that I wasn't there to be judgmental, but to help him as one brother to another. Then I asked, "Would you mind if I ask you some personal questions to see if we can identify the problem?"

Doug eagerly agreed. When our time together was over, we had pinpointed several causes for his struggle. He had known all about the Spirit-filled life; he had even taught it to several hundred Christians during the course of his ministry. But without realizing it, Doug had let himself become distracted. He had drifted away from some of the rich privileges God has made available to every Christian.

Disciplines for Spiritual Strength

Just as God has made eating an enjoyable discipline which we must partake of every day to stay strong, so has He provided several spiritual disciplines which we must exercise in order to stay spiritually strong and fruitful. If we approach these disciplines with a true desire to glorify our Lord, they actually become delightful experiences — privileges reserved strictly for members of His family.

However, if we get distracted or lazy and ignore these discipline-privileges, we can easily short-circuit the work the Holy Spirit wants to do through us. Like our fictional character Sam and my real-life friend Doug, we can drift into weakness and defeat.

In this chapter and the next, I want to share with you several "delightful disciplines" of the Christian life. I'll do so by reviewing the questions I asked Doug as we probed to see why he wasn't experiencing the joy of Spirit-filled living. I think you will find these questions helpful.

"Are you keeping short accounts with God?"

The psalmist wrote, "Search me, O God, and know my heart; test my thoughts. Point out anything you find in me that makes you sad, and lead me along the path of everlasting life" (Psalm 139:23,24).

I believe that this prayer is an essential discipline of the Christian's inner life. It expresses to God our desire for purity; our longing to make His ways our ways. Asking Him to reveal to us any unconfessed sin enables us to breathe spiritually and keep our accounts short with Him.

And think of it—what a privilege it is to seek God's personal help in living a life that will please Him!

We have already discussed Spiritual Breathing at length, so we will not go into further detail here. But let me suggest that you develop the discipline of ending each day with the psalmist's prayer. If the Holy Spirit reveals any unconfessed sin to you, deal with it on the spot, and fall asleep with the warm inner peace that all is right with your Lord.

"Are you taking good care of yourself physically?"

It is possible that a Christian who experiences unexplained lethargy is suffering from actual physical malnourishment. Our bodies are temples of the Holy Spirit (1 Corinthians 6:19), and if we let the temple deteriorate our emotional, mental and spiritual lives suffer as well.

While we are not to become preoccupied with our bodies, it is clear from the Scriptures that we are to take good care of ourselves. Often I have found that when a fellow Christian is struggling, the problem can be traced to poor sleeping patterns, too many refined sugars and junk foods, and lack of cardio-vascular activity. Any of these bad habits can deplete the energy we need to feel good and function effectively, and can lead to negative attitudes, weariness, and a lackadaisical spirit.

If you have not had a complete physical examination in some time, I encourage you to schedule one soon. Your physician may spot a problem area such as high blood pressure, low blood sugar, iron-poor blood, or high cholesterol levels that can be improved upon with his guidance.

When I asked Doug this question, he acknowledged that he had been getting only five hours' sleep at night when he really needed seven. It had been more than two months since his last jogging activity. I later found out that this was not the sole source of his problems, but I am sure that Doug's tired physical condition was a contributing factor.

"Are you totally committed to the Lordship of Christ?"

In recent decades the phrase *easy believism* has surfaced. Unfortunately, it describes a large number of contemporary Christians who have received Christ as Savior but do not, in practice, regard Him as Lord. They seem to have received Him in order to reach heaven someday or to get help for their problems, but they have never fully committed to trust, obey, honor and serve Him as a way of life.

Our Lord never intended that we be His casual acquaintances. He wants us to be His disciples, fully dedicated to following Him and lifting up His holy name to the world. We have already seen from Revelation 3 that our Lord is repulsed by mediocre commitment. "You don't realize that spiritually you are wretched and miserable and poor and blind and naked," He said to the fence-sitting Laodicean church. In John 14, Jesus explained why total obedience is so important to Him: "The one who obeys me is the one who loves me; and because he loves me, my

Father will love him; and I will too, and I will reveal myself to him . . . I will only reveal myself to those who love me and obey me . . . anyone who doesn't obey me doesn't love me" (John 14:21,23,24).

Webster's Third New International Dictionary tells us that the word *lord* signifies "one who has power and authority over others . . . a ruler by hereditary right or preeminence to whom service and obedience are due." When we acknowledge Christ as our Lord, we affirm that He is our Master for life and that we are dedicated to serving and glorifying Him. In all things, large and small, our deepest desire is to do what our Lord would want us to do. We ask for His guidance—not for our gain, but for His glory. We discipline ourselves in studying and obeying His written Word. We proclaim His love to the world around us. We try to think, speak and act in a way that will attract others to Him.

The misguided person who thinks all this is too difficult or irrelevant misses the point. The Christian life is far more than a fire escape from hell; it is the life of submission and obedience which result in joy and victory.

And what a privilege it is to submit to and obey the Lord of the universe! He knows everything past, present and future. He has walked before us, and walks beside us, to show us how to live lives of lasting significance and true fulfillment.

When I asked Doug if he remained fully committed to the Lordship of Christ, he squirmed a bit on the sofa. "I have made that commitment, sure. But I have to admit that recently I may not have been giving Christ first place in my life. I have become real busy and preoccupied with some projects and deadlines. Maybe I've been living more for myself than for His glory."

It is ironic but true that we well-meaning Christians

can sometimes become so busy trying to serve Christ that we fail to consult Him in the process. In our haste, we pass by the delights of life He has for us and we become preoccupied, tired and distant. In such times, we may actually do His kingdom more harm than good.

Other individuals may not be so well-intentioned. They live as though afraid that total commitment to Christ's Lordship will cause them to miss out on something desirable. So they hold back, hoping to find happiness and completion in other things, forgetting that Christ Himself equated mediocrity with misery and poverty. In real Christian life, mediocrity is misery; commitment is completion. Jesus said, "If you insist on saving your life, you will lose it. Only those who throw away their lives for my sake and for the sake of the Good News will ever know what it means to really live" (Mark 8:35).

So Doug and I had identified another trouble spot. He had been disregarding one foundational discipline (and privilege) of Spirit-filled living: complete and ongoing commitment to Christ's Lordship. Christ is the Master; we are His servants dedicated to knowing, loving and serving Him.

If you haven't already done so, let me encourage you to dedicate yourself to following Him moment by moment, day by day. Then, every morning and evening in prayer, acknowledge Him as your Lord and commit to obeying Him for His glory. The Holy Spirit will help you do so.

"Is your first love still first?"

In Revelation, we find a church of hard-working, obedient Christians. Nothing lukewarm about the church in Ephesus! Chapter 2 records Jesus' acknowledgment of their "toil and perseverance," that they "cannot endure evil men," that they put false prophets to the test. Jesus commended them for the fact that they "have endured for My name's sake, and have not grown weary."

Yet there was a serious problem with this group of believers. Jesus said to them, "But I have this against you, that *you have left your first love*" (2:4).

The first-generation Ephesian church had been commended for its love for God and others (Ephesians 3:17-19). But now, the second generation had become so busy *doing things* for God that they had lost their intimacy with Him. They had "left their first love."

It's kind of like a marriage relationship today. When you married your spouse, you were deeply "in love." You couldn't spend enough time with him or get enough of him. Because of your love, you wanted to do everything possible to please him.

But for sake of illustration, let's say that eventually you became so busy doing the things that please your spouse that you did not have any time to spend in quiet togetherness with him, to keep the love burning bright. Of course you still love him, but the quality of love you once had for him is faded.

He asks, "Do you love me as much as you once did?" You say "yes," but he can tell you do not. Before, you wanted to do all these things because of your deep love for him. Now, you're just going through the motions because it's the thing to do when you're married. Does this hurt him? Of course.

This is what Jesus saw in the second-generation Ephesian Christians. Earlier, He had summarized what He meant by "first love" in Matthew 22:37-38: "Love the Lord your God with all your heart, soul, and mind." The Ephesians described in Revelation kept busy, and did many good things, but they were motivated more by legalism than by their love for God and for others.

In modern day, it is just as easy for us to become so involved in the activities of Christian ministry that we drift away from loving the Lord our God with all our heart, soul and mind. Our good deeds are worthless if not motivated by a deep and sincere love for Him.

When I asked Doug this question, he was reluctant to admit that he had left his first love. "Yes," he admitted finally, "I guess I have been on a downslide lately. To be honest, I've been motivated by getting the job done, rather than by my love for the Lord. I need to get my motives right again."

"How is your prayer life?"

We have the amazing privilege of talking directly with the omnipotent God. He is more accessible to us than our doctor or dentist! We don't need to set up a five-minute appointment for three weeks from Friday, nor is there any time limit on our conversations with Him. He is always there, always ready to listen. Prayer is one of the ways God has provided for us to seek His mind and know His will.

Dwight L. Moody said, "The Christian on his knees sees more than the philosopher on tiptoe." Thus, prayer is a key discipline for the Christian who wants to live with purpose and power.

Doug realized that in recent weeks his prayer life had deteriorated from intimate conversations to quick "sky telegrams" delivered on the run. "Thanks for this food, bless us today," he would pray before crunching down his morning cereal. "Lord, please give us the money we need," he would murmur when a larger-than-expected bill arrived in the mail. "Lord, give me a good night's sleep" was his supplication as he dropped exhausted into bed just before midnight.

"Doug, you have three busy children," I observed. "How would you feel if the only time they talked with you was to say, 'Dad, gimme ten dollars,' as they rushed out the door?"

"I see your point," my friend smiled. "I would feel used. Like they didn't really love *me*, but only looked on me as a money supply. I imagine my recent prayer patterns have come across that way to God."

God does want us to come to Him with our needs. But He desires a closer, more intimate communion with His children that goes far deeper than a wish list. Unhurried prayer—in which we praise and thank God, intercede for others, ask for His wisdom and listen for His guidance— demonstrates our love for Him and our desire to seek His mind in all things. Jesus exercised the daily discipline of communication with His heavenly Father; He was the Son of God, yet He made prayer top priority! Prayer renewed His strength and nurtured His intimacy with the Father. It can do the same for us.

In his letters to early Christians, the apostle Paul emphasized the importance of ongoing prayer:

> "Pray all the time. Ask God for anything according to the Holy Spirit's wishes" (Ephesians 6:18).
> "Don't be weary in prayer; keep at it; watch for God's answers and remember to be thankful when they come" (Colossians 4:2).
> "Always keep on praying" (1 Thessalonians 5:17).

I count myself fortunate that I learned early in my Christian life about the privilege of prayer. Over the years I have made a point to be on my knees in prayer last thing at night before slipping into bed, and first thing in the morning as I get out of bed. In this way, my first and last thoughts each day are of my wonderful Savior and Lord. His peace fills me as I cast all my cares on Him and bask in His love and goodness.

Throughout the day, I try to begin each meeting with

prayer. Frequently, my associates and I will pray together in my office, in the hallway, on the telephone and before and after meetings. And several times each day I commit a question or project to God, because I know that unless I am yielded to His will all my efforts can be worthless.

Prayer *is* a discipline—but it is also a matchless privilege! According to Philippians 4:6, God wants us to talk to Him about *everything*.

Please do not treat lightly the discipline and privilege of prayer. Just as unrushed, in-depth conversation with a spouse or friend draws you closer to that person, so will unhurried and honest conversation with God draw you nearer to Him.

"Have you been spending adequate time in God's Word?"

Another nourishing delight God has made available to us is His written Word, the Holy Bible. Someone has aptly described it as "God's love letter to His children," in which we find reliable history, practical guidance, and powerful glimpses of God—all woven together by the story of our redemption through the death of our Lord Jesus Christ on the cross for our sins.

When I think of the riches of this Book, I am embarrassed that I do not invest even more time studying and memorizing it. Many Christians, sadly, virtually ignore it—even to the point of neglecting to open the Bible and follow along as the pastor reads from it on Sunday mornings.

If you own a Bible, you possess a priceless treasure. Read what others have said about this Book:

> The Bible was never intended to be a book for scholars and specialists only. From the very beginning it was intended to be everybody's Book, and that is what it continues to be.
> —F. F. Bruce

The Bible is an inexhaustible fountain of all truths. The existence of the Bible is the greatest blessing which humanity ever experienced.

—Immanuel Kant

All the good from the Savior of the world is communicated through this Book. All the things desirable to man are contained in it.

· —Abraham Lincoln

I did not go through the Book. The Book went through me.

—A. W. Tozer

The truly wise man is he who believes the Bible against the opinions of any man. If the Bible says one thing, and any body of men says another, the wise man will decide, "This Book is the Word of Him who cannot lie."

—R. A. Torrey

If God is a reality, and the soul is a reality, and you are an immortal being, what are you doing with your Bible shut?

—Herrick Johnson

How tragic that this personal love letter from God often gathers dust in our homes! Through the centuries, men and women have given their lives to preserve this Book. In recent years and today, Christians in totalitarian nations have longed for a complete copy of their own and have risked their lives to receive it. Yet, too many of us in freer countries take God's Word for granted and fail to fill our minds and hearts with its incredibly relevant and practical guidance.

God's Word is a discipline-privilege which has been among the most forsaken by today's believers, and for our complacency we are paying the price of ignorance. Ignorance of God's truth leads to compromise, which leads to carnality, which leads to spiritual impotence and often to gross sin.

"How can a young man keep his way pure? By keeping it according to Thy word," the psalmist noted. "Thy word I have treasured in my heart, That I might not sin against Thee" (Psalm 119:9,11, NAS).

Doug and I discovered that during the past few weeks, his only time in the Word had been on Sunday mornings at church. We agreed that He would set aside twenty to thirty minutes before breakfast each day to read and meditate on a portion of the Bible. He established a goal of memorizing at least one new verse of Scripture every two weeks and reviewing these verses on a regular basis.

If you have not been investing regular, quality time in the riches of God's Word, I urge you to do so, beginning today! Use a modern-day translation or paraphrase. You might want to use *The One-Year Bible* or a devotional guide such as my book *Promises: A Daily Guide to Supernatural Living* to direct your reading and study.

Begin memorizing key Scriptures that are especially meaningful to you. As you think on these Scriptures, praise and thank God for His abundant promises. As temptations or difficult situations arise, the Holy Spirit will bring these verses to mind to strengthen and help you.

The author of the first psalm painted a beautiful word picture of how meditating on God's Word brings power and peace:

> They [those who delight in God's Word] are like trees along a river bank bearing luscious fruit each season without fail. Their leaves shall never wither, and all they do shall prosper (Psalm 1:3).

"Have you been living by faith?"

"You can never please God without faith, without

depending on him," the author of Hebrews wrote (11:6). Earlier in that same chapter, he provided an excellent working definition of faith:

> What is faith? It is the confident assurance that something we want is going to happen. It is the certainty that what we hope for is waiting for us, even though we cannot see it up ahead (Hebrews 11:1).

Without faith, it is impossible to please God. He expects us to trust Him to work all things together for good, even though we may not be able to imagine how our circumstances could possibly work out for good! He wants us to love others by faith, knowing that He is filling us with His supernatural, unconditional love. He wants us to tell others about Him in faith that the Holy Spirit will work behind the scenes to draw the listener into God's kingdom in His own timing. As Oswald Chambers wrote, "Faith never knows where it is being led, but it loves and knows the One who is leading."

How do we develop this faith and live by it? Dwight L. Moody tells how he discovered the principle of living by faith:

> I prayed for faith and thought that some day faith would come down and strike me like lightning. But faith did not seem to come. One day I read in the tenth chapter of Romans, "Faith cometh by hearing, and hearing by the Word of God." I had [up to this time] closed my Bible and prayed for faith. I now opened my Bible and began to study, and faith has been growing ever since.

How is your faith? Do you live with the quiet inner peace that comes from knowing God loves you, that He indeed has your best interest at heart, that He empowers you to do the work He has called you to do?

*"Have you been keeping praise in your heart
and on your lips?"*

In an earlier chapter I shared with you how a constant attitude of praise has helped me get my eyes off my limited capabilities and onto my all-powerful Lord. What a difference this practice has made in my life!

Do not make the mistake of thinking, as some skeptics do, that praise is a Pollyanna way of avoiding reality. Rather, praise is how we are to *confront* reality. The Psalms exhort us to praise God in all things. The apostle Paul, in Philippians 4:4-8, wrote that the way to deal with real life is to dwell on the positive:

> Always be full of joy in the Lord; I say it again, rejoice!
>
> . . . Fix your thoughts on what is true and good and right. Think about things that are pure and lovely, and dwell on the fine, good things in others. Think about all you can praise God for and be glad about.

What is praise? A friend of mine defines it as *Giving credit where credit is due.* I like that. As we walk through each day, we have the privilege of acknowledging to God and to others how majestic, gracious and loving our God is.

Praise isn't always easy; and that is why it is also a discipline. Harold Lindsell says that "the continual offering of praise requires stamina; we ought to praise God even when we do not feel like it. Praising Him takes away the blues and restores us to normal."

If praise has not been a constant part of your life, let me share some suggestions to help you enjoy the blessings of this discipline.

First, memorize and meditate on God's Word, especially the praise passages found in Psalms. As you dwell on these Scriptures, thank God that His promises and provisions are just as real now as they were when the Scriptures were written.

Second, invest in several of the praise music cassettes at your Christian bookstore. On these tapes, Christian musicians have taken key praise Scriptures and put them to song. As you learn the songs, you also learn the Scriptures and can sing them silently or aloud wherever you go. As you sing, focus your thoughts on the Lord and what He means to you.

Third, in any situation, good or bad, learn to ask the question, *Who is sovereign here?* Here is how it works:

> You're taking a walk and revelling in the beauty around you. A crisp blue sky with cotton-ball clouds. A warm breeze whispering through the trees. An inspiring sunset. Ask: *Who is sovereign here?* Who made this? Then acknowledge that God is the loving Creator who provided this "canvas" for you to enjoy.
>
> You're working on a tight deadline for a church project when you learn that someone has dropped the ball and the project is in jeopardy. Ask: *Who is sovereign here?* God is still in charge, and this question will remind you to stop and praise Him, despite the circumstances. The benefit is that the act of praise will calm your spirit as you take your eyes off your limited resources and focus on God's limitless resources. Praise demonstrates your faith, which pleases God and results in the release of His wisdom, love and power on your behalf.

Fourth, begin every prayer with a period of adoration of your wonderful Lord, thanking Him who He is, for His attributes, and for the things He has done in your life.

If worship has not been a regular part of your day, let me encourage you to discover the supernatural power and peace that come from praise! As you exercise the discipline of praising God in the midst of *every* situation, the joy of the Holy Spirit will fill you. You will be able to move forward with a clear mind and a positive spirit, fully enjoying the adventure of trusting God.

FOR REFLECTION, DISCUSSION AND ACTION

1. Read the quote by Henry Drummond at the beginning of this chapter. Do you agree or disagree with him? Why? Support your answer from Scripture.

2. What discipline-privileges of the inner life have brought you the greatest enjoyment? How, specifically, have you found them helpful in your everyday life?

3. What discipline-privileges have been weak spots in your Christian walk? Why do you think you have failed to fully enjoy them? In what ways has this affected your attitudes, actions and effectiveness for Christ?

4. In the past, have you generally regarded these discipline-privileges as drudgery or delight? Explain your answer. After studying this chapter, what attitude do you want to take toward these inner disciplines? Why?

5. Review each of the discipline-privileges of this chapter, honestly asking yourself each question. Before God, commit to making each discipline an integral part of your life. By faith, trust the Holy Spirit to remind and empower you to do so.

11

*Delightful
Disciplines of the
Outward Life*

> *A cross Christian, an anxious Christian, a dis-
> couraged, gloomy Christian, a doubting Christian, a
> complaining Christian, an exacting Christian, a self-
> ish Christian, a cruel, hard-hearted Christian, a self-
> indulgent Christian, a Christian with a sharp tongue
> or bitter spirit—all these may be very earnest in their
> work, and may have honorable places in the church;
> but they are not Christlike Christians.*
> *Hannah Whitall Smith*

The alarm ripped through Sam's restless dreams. It was
the morning after his crackers-and-water dinner at the
Hungry Man Smorgasbord, and as he pulled his weary
bones from the bed he muttered, "I can't believe it's morning already."

He stumbled to the bathroom sink. "You look awful,"

he muttered to the apparition in the mirror. He *felt* awful. In the past few weeks he had barely eaten—oh, he'd grabbed a Twinkie here, a bag of potato chips there—but for some reason he just had not found the time to sit down and partake of a good meal. Things were busy at work, and at the end of the day there had been errands to run, repairs to make, hobbies to pursue and TV programs to watch. Each night for the past few weeks he had either driven right past the Hungry Man Smorgasbord or, like last night, gone through the line too hastily and eaten only crackers and water.

On his way out the door, Sam opened the refrigerator and reached past the bacon, eggs and orange juice for a five-day-old doughnut. This would be his breakfast—and lunch—for the day. He'd stop at the Hungry Man again tonight, if he had time.

At the office, Sam's cohorts exchanged intelligence reports among themselves. "Watch out for Sam today," John cautioned. "He looks grumpy again."

"Looks?" rejoined Sara. "Take my word for it—he *is* grumpy. This morning he was short with me. He even said some sarcastic things about the brochure I did for him!"

"He sure hasn't been much fun to be around lately," Barbara added. "I plan to avoid him as much as possible."

Sam knew he was unhappy. He just didn't feel the inner vitality he once enjoyed. He wasn't getting his work done. He didn't want to be around people, and when he was around them he didn't care what he said or did. He felt tired and obnoxious, but he couldn't figure out why . . .

"You know," my friend Doug realized, "I've had this inner turmoil inside me, and I think I'm discovering why. I *know* all this stuff—I know I need to keep Christ first, spend time with Him in prayer and Bible study, and praise

Him continuously. But I haven't been doing it."

As Doug and I continued our visit in my office, we realized that the reason he had felt so restless was that the Holy Spirit had been urging him to get back to the inner disciplines of the Spirit-filled walk, and Doug had been ignoring Him. "I haven't obeyed His leading," he said in a tone of personal discovery. "So I took a double hit: I starved myself of the joy and strength I could have gained through these disciplines, and I added the sin of disobedience on top of it all. No wonder I've been worthless the past few weeks!"

At Doug's request, we paused to pray together. In a beautifully simple prayer, my friend confessed his disobedience and appropriated God's forgiveness and cleansing. When we finished, Doug looked as if a load of bricks had been lifted from his shoulders. "It was all so basic," he shook his head in amazement. "I just got so busy and burned out that I didn't see what was happening."

As Doug spoke, he realized something else.

"You know, during these weeks I haven't been much of a witness. My wife told me I haven't been smiling much, and I know I've been moody and impatient with my co-workers and with my kids. I haven't been very interested in helping others.

"It seems there are several *outward* disciplines, too, which are closely tied to the inner disciplines. Ignoring the inner disciplines drained me of the inner strength and joy I need in order to be Christlike around others."

Our Visible Witness to Others

Doug had hit upon a crucial point. Just as there are *inner* discipline-privileges of the Spirit-filled life that help us grow in our faith and intimacy with God, so are there *outward* discipline-privileges that help us enjoy life and present a positive visible witness to the world around us.

And the two are closely interrelated. If we ignore the inner life, the outward life will suffer. Our fictional friend Sam had failed for several weeks to dine upon the abundant cuisine available to him, and now he just didn't have the strength or desire to smile or share a kind word with others. My friend Doug had failed to renew his strength in prayer, Bible study and the other inner discipline-privileges, and as a result he had been less cheerful and courteous in his dealings with other people.

We have the privilege of being our Lord's ambassadors to the world. The way we act and speak in public may be the only picture of Jesus Christ some people ever see. Do we live, speak and act in such a way that others will want to know our Lord too? Or do we repel them from the Savior because the fruit of the Spirit is not evident in our outward lives?

Ambassadorship is a privilege, but it is a discipline. With the Holy Spirit's help from within, we need to consciously think about how our visible lives reflect upon our Lord Jesus Christ.

Doug and I took a few more minutes to highlight some of the discipline-privileges of the outward life — practices that will help every Christian enjoy his relationships with others and honor God by his words and deeds.

"Do you reflect Christ in your countenance?"

"A happy face means a glad heart; a sad face means a breaking heart," says Proverbs 15:13.

Your countenance includes your facial expressions, body language and overall attitude — all working together. In other words, is there one big smile radiating outward? Do people see joy in your eyes, in your smile, in the way you sit and walk, in your energy level?

As the saying goes, "A picture is worth a thousand

words." A joyful expression testifies that Christ is on the throne of your life and that He is your partner and guide in whatever challenges the day may bring. A dull countenance announces that something is wrong inside.

As people observe your countenance, what picture are they seeing? What "thousand words" are formulating in their minds about how you've learned to handle life?

Communication experts tell us that one's expressions, body language and attitudes convey what is really going on inside an individual. The individual may use words to cover up his true feelings. I have known Christians with dour countenances who try to do just that, and if it weren't so sad it would be humorous. "I'm so joyful that Christ is my Savior and Lord," one might say with lifeless eyes and not even the trace of a smile. "It's so wonderful to be filled with the Spirit and experience His love, joy and peace . . ." another will add with a somber expression as he slouches in his chair.

People draw quick conclusions from the pictures they see, and if they observe a weary or hostile countenance they are likely to conclude that we do not possess the inner resources to handle life. Therefore, it is important that we exercise the discipline-privilege of a joyful countenance.

Ask God to remind you, through His Holy Spirit, to reflect energy, joy and vitality in your physical mannerisms:

- a confident smile
- a joyful, confident facial expression
- good posture
- a spring in your step
- a friendly greeting and look in the eye for everyone

"Do your words honor Jesus Christ?"

Jerry, who has been a Christian for more than twenty years, is talented, energetic and humorous.

But he has a blind spot. He loves to make off-color remarks. He rarely tells an actual dirty joke, but his quick wit often plays on words to produce sexual innuendos that enthrall some people and embarrass others.

Janet is also a Christian wanting to live as she should. She understands the Spirit-filled life and wants to introduce others to Christ.

But she has a problem. When she hears a piece of juicy gossip, she can't keep it quiet. In the blink of an eye, she's on the phone to a friend to pass it along. Oftentimes she subconsciously tries to sanctify the gossip by presenting it in the form of a prayer request: "Mary, be sure to pray for Sue. I've heard reports that she might be sleeping around with several men."

We have the privilege of honoring our Lord Jesus Christ with our words. They can reflect His goodness within.

Just as easily, we can dishonor Him with our words. Like Jerry's or Janet's, our words can grieve Him, hurt our fellow believers, and ruin our witness to non-Christians around us.

God's Word has several strong messages for us about what we say. Here are just a few:

> If anyone can control his tongue, it proves that he has perfect control over himself in every other way . . . the tongue is a small thing, but what enormous damage it can do (James 3:2,5).

> May my spoken words and unspoken thoughts be pleasing even to you, O Lord my Rock and my Redeemer (Psalm 19:14).

A good man's speech reveals the rich treasures within him. An evil-hearted man is filled with venom, and his speech reveals it. And I tell you this, that you must give account on Judgment Day for every idle word you speak (Matthew 12:35,36).

A friend of mine who had struggled with a life-long habit of foul language told me of the progress he had made in this critical area. "Each morning in prayer," he reported, "I would consciously give Christ control of the throne of my life. And I would pray, 'Lord, if I think of anything to say that would not be pleasing in Your sight, please stop me before I say it.' "

Through the Holy Spirit, my friend found himself pausing in that split second between thinking and speaking, and determining that an expression was not Christlike.

"Then, as a next step, I started praying each morning, 'Lord, help me to not even *think* those words that would be displeasing to You.' It has taken time, and I've fallen a few times, but He is changing my thought life from within."

The indwelling power of the Holy Spirit, combined with the discipline of pausing to think before he spoke, helped clean up his thought life as well as his actual words.

Let us not abuse the privilege we have of representing Jesus Christ by our words. Let us exercise the discipline to avoid unedifying or hurtful talk, and consciously seek to encourage and build up one another by what we say.

"Are your actions Christlike?"

A pained expression came to Doug's eyes as he realized that some of his recent actions had not glorified Christ in the eyes of his wife and children.

"I've been impatient with Julie, who wanted me to slow down and spend more time with her and the kids," he admitted. "And when the kids wanted me to do something with them, I had to keep telling them 'no.' A couple of times they were just being their lively selves, but I simply couldn't handle it—I grew angry and yelled at them."

Doug thought for a moment. "The worst thing I could do to my kids is preach the joyful Christian life but not live it. I have some apologizing to do at home."

While the selection of words is important to our visible witness, our actions speak even more loudly. Jim, a deacon at church and active in the choir, always has a bright smile, a hearty handshake and a funny story on Sundays and during social events. But at his appliance store, he's another person. With his employees, Jim is gruff and impatient. On more than one occasion he has thrown a tool angrily when a repair hasn't gone right. What kind of visible witness is Jim presenting to his employees?

"The serene, silent beauty of a holy life is the most powerful influence in the world, next to the might of God," wrote Blaise Pascal, the French physicist-philosopher.

Are your actions Christlike? Let us commit ourselves to the joyful discipline of honoring Jesus Christ by our actions. We should always act as though He is right there beside us, watching everything we do. Why? Because He *is* there—and He has promised never to leave or forsake us.

He has entrusted to us the privilege of modeling His likeness to others by our actions. And our success in this discipline will depend to a large extent on our answer to the next question . . .

"Are you others-centered?"

This discipline-privilege is fundamental to Christlike words and actions. The apostle Paul made it clear that God wants us to be vitally interested in the welfare of others:

Don't be selfish; don't live to make a good impression on others. Be humble, thinking of others as better than yourself. Don't just think about your own affairs, but be interested in others, too, and in what they are doing (Philippians 2:3,4).

In dozens of other passages, God's Word teaches the importance of *agape* love. This love is others-centered. It is a fruit of the Holy Spirit's work in our lives, but we must make a conscious decision, moment by moment, to express that love in our words and actions. That's the discipline and the privilege of being others-centered.

Curt and Alice have discovered the delightful discipline of being others-centered. As they keep Christ on the throne of their lives, the Holy Spirit guides them toward everyday opportunities to demonstrate love in action.

Last week they learned that Alice's friend Marie had lost her job. Within an hour, they were at Marie's door with a pizza and two bags of groceries. Curt and Alice spent the entire evening listening to, encouraging and praying with their friend. They have called their network of business acquaintances to check job openings, and have helped line up several promising interviews for Marie.

Ted's neighbor George was hauling six cubic yards of topsoil from his driveway to his backyard garden. Six cubic yards doesn't sound like much until you've tried to haul it yourself, one wheelbarrow at a time. Ted had some activities planned for the day, but when he saw George working alone he empathized with his neighbor and wanted to lend a hand.

Now Ted didn't exactly get up that Saturday morning thinking, *If only I could spend the morning shoveling dirt into my wheelbarrow, hauling it to the backyard, and dumping it—that would make my day!* It was others-centered love, produced by the Holy Spirit and put into action through a conscious decision on Ted's part, that made him want to help.

"Good morning, Neighbor!" Ted called to George as he pushed his own wheelbarrow over to George's driveway. "Could you use some help?"

Of course, George told Ted he really didn't need to get dirty hauling the topsoil. "Hey, I could use the exercise," Ted countered. "Besides, it looks like two of us could make it go much faster. When we're done, Katie's got a pitcher of cold iced tea waiting for us."

In the two hours they spent hauling soil, Ted and George became better acquainted as they talked about football, jobs and family. When Ted's wife Katie brought the iced tea over, they invited George and his wife to their home for dinner the following Saturday. It was the start of a lasting friendship, and several weeks later Ted and Katie were able to take their neighbors to church and eventually help them receive Christ as their Savior and Lord.

Watch for those opportunities — big and small — to put love into action. It truly is a privilege to put others first, and our genuine desire to encourage, help, care for and share with others will offer a living portrait of Christlikeness to those with whom we come in contact.

"Are you spiritually accountable to someone?"

The importance of this discipline-privilege has come under the spotlight in recent years, as several nationally known Christian leaders and dozens of pastors have become involved in illicit sexual relationships. As a result, they have dishonored our Lord, disgraced their families, and sabotaged their ministries.

No matter how long we have walked with Christ or how diligently we have served Him, none of us are exempt from the assaults of Satan.

In earlier chapters we have seen how the Christian still has two natures within him, the Flesh and the Spirit. Every day we are bombarded with messages from Satan's kingdom—temptations as deceptive and alluring as the apple was to Eve in the Garden of Eden. With Jesus Christ in our lives, we do not have to be slaves to Satan's messages—we have the freedom and power to choose to listen to the wise, healthful messages from God's kingdom. But choose we must, for God has granted us free agency.

Because we have a fallen, sinful nature and God has given us the freedom to choose, we are susceptible to sin. The Christian who denies susceptibility is only fooling himself and is a likely candidate for a prideful fall.

One very effective strategy to help us stay strong is the discipline of accountability to fellow Christians. Here's how it works: Find one or more fellow believers of your gender whom you trust. Commit to meet together regularly to encourage and pray for one another as you challenge each other to spiritual growth and purity. If you find yourself struggling with temptation, call a member of your group to ask for prayer and discussion.

Of course, honesty, humility and confidentiality are vital to the success of such a group. But knowing that you are being held accountable by a fellow Christian who is interested in your spiritual success can give you strength and guidance in the face of the enemy's assaults.

My good friend Ted Engstrom shares what such a commitment has meant to him:

> Many years ago I heard [a] friend of mine, Pastor Ray Stedman, talk about a special group of men he had gathered to meet with him on a weekly basis. These men were not all members of his congregation, but were close friends who held each other accountable in the spiritual walk. He said his experience with that small group was one of the most meaningful in his life.

After thinking about it, and realizing the need for such accountability in my own life, I talked to my pastor about it. Dr. Ray Ortland was interested. He expressed similar deep needs and feelings, so we met a couple of times to discuss the concept. Then we invited several men to meet with us. Some of the original group dropped out, but ultimately there were six of us who met together periodically for more than ten years in a local restaurant. We called it the 2/4/6 Club, indicating that there were six of us, who met on the second and fourth Friday mornings of each month for breakfast.

It was not a prayer group—although we did pray together. It was not a Bible study group—although we did spend time in the Word. It was a time of meeting and growing together, appreciating each other and sharing our spiritual pilgrimages. There was no appointed leader and no agenda. We met to share experiences, to laugh and to weep. We rejoiced in our successes. We also shared and were open about our failures.

Those meetings have literally changed my life.[1]

Let me encourage you to form an accountability partnership with one or more Christians whom you trust. Commit to pray for, encourage, correct, and help one another in living the Spirit-controlled life. Do so with a spirit of gentleness and humility, but be totally honest when sharing your struggles and when correcting each other.

As Ted Engstrom says, "We need help from each other. About the only thing we can do well by ourselves is fail."

"Are you sharing Christ with others?"

Disobeying God is a sure way to be miserable, weak and ineffective. Yet, many Christians ignore the fact that this discipline-privilege is a specific command given us by our Lord Jesus Christ.

Although the very thought of witnessing causes many

Christians' knees to shake, helping others find new life in Christ is without question the greatest privilege God grants us. Because I believe that sharing Christ with others is so important to a Christian's happiness, I have devoted this book's entire last chapter to the subject.

As Doug and I concluded our visit, he admitted that he had recently passed up several clear opportunities to tell someone what Christ meant to him. He knew how to share his faith effectively, but his failure in several of the inner disciplines had dissipated his desire to obey God in this vital area.

We again prayed together, trusting God to restore Doug to his first love for our Lord. Doug asked God to enable him, through the fullness of the Holy Spirit, to be diligent in exercising the discipline-privileges of the Spirit-filled life.

I'm happy to report that the zeal has returned to Doug's life. His joyful countenance is back, as contagious as before, and he is more effective than ever in his family life and personal ministry.

You, too, can keep the energy and joy alive in your walk with God by dining regularly at His feast of delightful disciplines. He has provided them in love, to help us enjoy Him, grow in Him, and live with purpose and power. We have a clear choice: We can ignore them, and suffer inevitable weakness, complacency and defeat. Or we can partake, and experience the promise of Isaiah 40:31:

> They that wait upon the Lord
> shall renew their strength.
> they shall mount up with wings like eagles;
> they shall run and not be weary;
> they shall walk and not faint.

FOR REFLECTION, DISCUSSION AND ACTION

1. Read the quote by Hannah Whitall Smith at the beginning of this chapter. Do you agree or disagree with her? Why? Support your answer from Scripture and share some real-life examples.

2. What discipline-privileges of the outward life have brought you the greatest enjoyment? Share a recent example of how a particular discipline helped you demonstrate God's love to someone.

3. What discipline-privileges of the outward life have been weak spots in your Christian experience? Why do you think you have failed to fully enjoy them? In what ways do you think this has affected your visible witness to others and/or your effectiveness for Christ?

4. In the past, have you generally regarded these outward disciplines as drudgery or delight? Explain your answer. After studying this chapter, what attitude do you want to have toward these outward disciplines? Why?

5. Review each of the discipline-privileges of this chapter, honestly asking yourself each question. With God's help, commit yourself to making each discipline an integral part of your life. By faith, trust the Holy Spirit to remind and empower you to do so.

---

1. Ted W. Engstrom, *Integrity* (Dallas, TX: Word Books, 1987) quoted by Robert C. Larson in *The Best of Ted Engstrom* (San Bernardino, CA: Here's Life Publishers, 1988), pp. 35-36.

Of all the feasts at God's table,
this one is by far the most gratifying.

12

The Greatest Privilege of All

You shall receive power when the Holy Spirit has come upon you; and you shall be My witnesses both in Jerusalem, and in all Judea and Samaria, and even to the remotest part of the earth.

Jesus Christ
Acts 1:8, NAS

When wise and benevolent people know they are about to be separated from the ones they love, they often save their most important words till last.

These are the words they want us to remember when they are gone—the words that sum up their lives and offer wisdom, comfort and direction to those of us left behind.

The last recorded words of our Lord's visit to Earth are like that. Of all the things He could have said to us before ascending to heaven, He chose to make the statement recorded in Acts 1:8. His final words were of promise, privilege and priority.

The promise: *You shall receive power when the Holy Spirit has come upon you.* Jesus knew that God's Holy Spirit would come to reside in us when we received Him, filling us with the power we need to live the Christian life and share His love with others.

The privilege: *and you shall be My witnesses both in Jerusalem, and in all Judea and Samaria, and even to the remotest part of the earth.* Our Lord Jesus Christ has granted us the privilege of personally representing Him, to help others understand His love and forgiveness and His provision for their eternity.

The priority: The author of Acts reports that "after [Jesus] had said these things, He was lifted up while they were looking on, and a cloud received Him out of their sight" (1:9, NAS). By making these His last words to us, Jesus underscored the priority He places on sharing the Good News with others. These are our marching orders! Theologians have since called this passage, along with Matthew 28:18-20 and Mark 16:15,16, "The Great Commission."

The Unused Privilege

Of all the discipline-privileges of the Spirit-filled life, telling others about our Lord is the most gratifying and fulfilling. Think of it! The Lord Jesus Christ has honored *us* with the privilege of sharing His message with men, women, boys and girls who do not yet know Him. He has selected *us* (of all methods He could have chosen) as His personal representatives! We have the matchless opportunity to take part in rescuing men and women from Satan's kingdom and bringing them into God's kingdom.

Wherever I have traveled over the years, I have asked Christians two questions. The first, "What is the most important thing that has ever happened to you?" invariably brings the response, "Receiving Jesus Christ as my Savior and Lord." Then I ask, "In light of that, what is the most important thing you can do with your life?" Again, almost invariably, the answer is "Tell others how they can receive Christ, too!"

Yet, sadly, sharing our faith in Christ is probably the most disobeyed discipline-privilege of the Christian life. We know we should witness to others, for we hear it from the pulpit and read about it in our Bibles. And every one of us can remember those awkward moments with a friend or acquaintance when a small voice inside us seemed to whisper, *Tell him about Jesus. Tell him!* But we froze, smiled timidly, and changed the subject.

Many of us have never told another person about the most important thing that has ever happened in our lives. We would rather talk about anything else: TV or movies, sports, the job, the children, even politics. But when it comes to obeying our Lord's final command and talking about "the most joyful news ever announced" (Luke 2:10), many of us suddenly become tongue-tied.

Three Reasons Why We Don't Share Our Faith

Why is it that we Christians can talk about practically anything with anyone, but we shrink back when the opportunity arises to tell others about the new life they can find in Christ?

I have found that there are three primary reasons: lack of interest, lack of courage, and lack of practical know-how. All three can be traced to our not being directed and empowered by the Holy Spirit.

Lack of Interest

The Christian who has little interest in witnessing reveals that he also has little interest in the welfare of others, for God's Word clearly teaches that those who do not receive Christ face an eternity of spiritual separation from God. John the Baptist said of Jesus: "All who trust him — God's Son — to save them have eternal life; those who don't believe and obey him shall never see heaven, but the wrath of God remains upon them" (John 3:36). The apostle Paul affirmed this teaching in Romans 6:23: "For the wages of sin is death, but the free gift of God is eternal life through Jesus Christ our Lord."

If we genuinely love others, we are compelled by that love to want the best for them. We want to help them turn away from sin and accept the gift of eternal life. Therefore, a lack of interest in telling others about Christ is a lack of love, and if love is not present we are not allowing the Holy Spirit to control our lives. Carnality has drained away the desire to obey God and help another person find new life.

Nearly every day, Chuck encountered men and women who did not know Christ. Several had become good friends. But despite spending hours together, Chuck had never shared with any of them what Jesus Christ could do in their lives. He didn't want to upset them, and besides, he wasn't really sure what Christ meant in *his own* life at the time.

"But when I learned that most Christians are carnal, I realized why I had no interest in telling my friends about Jesus," Chuck recalls. On several fronts, including witnessing, he had been disobedient. He had failed to keep short accounts with God, and as a result Christ was not on the throne of his life — Chuck was. He didn't have the love of the Holy Spirit coming from within.

"Let's face it — if one of my friends had had terminal cancer, and I knew the cure, I would have told him how to cure his cancer," Chuck admits. "But these same friends, who didn't know Jesus, had the worst kind of cancer — the cancer of sin, of living without God. But I didn't have the kind of love that wanted the best for them spiritually."

Chuck went through the Spiritual Breathing procedure, trusting God to fill him with *agape* love for his friends. "That made the difference," he says. "With the Holy Spirit in control, I really began to care about my friends on the spiritual level. I was a little nervous at first, but I prayed for strength and started to gently encourage my friends to consider Jesus Christ.

"A few have received Him, and several others seem interested in considering what I've said. I don't think any of them think less of me for sharing with them, but even if they did it would be worth it.

"The bottom line is, if I really love others, I will want what is best for them — and knowing Jesus Christ is *always* the best thing that could happen to them!"

Have you felt little interest in sharing your faith? The Holy Spirit can fill you with loving concern for others! "For God has not given us a spirit of timidity, but of power and love and discipline" (2 Timothy 1:7, NAS).

Lack of Courage

I confess: I have personally felt every fear and considered every excuse invented for not witnessing. Talking with others about our Lord does not always come easily for me. So if fear has been your obstacle in witnessing, I can empathize with you. It's natural to feel a little nervous, especially in your initial attempts to witness for Christ. I sure did, and I have shared many of my experiences, warts and all, in my recent book *Witnessing Without Fear: How to Share Your Faith With Confidence.*

But for almost forty years now, the Holy Spirit has enabled me to go beyond my shyness and fear and enjoy the discipline-privilege of sharing the Good News wherever I go. He will do the same for you!

Think for a moment on the Flesh vs. Spirit diagram I

shared earlier in this book. If you are receiving messages of fear, from whom are they coming?

"We wrestle not against flesh and blood, but against principalities, against powers, against the rulers of the darkness of this world," Ephesians 6 tells us.

There is a definite spiritual battle raging. Satan wants to rob you of the joy of sharing Christ, and he wants to rob the other person of the joy of knowing Christ. So when you sense the Holy Spirit leading you to tell someone about Jesus, Satan's agents go to work filling you with morbid visions of embarrassment and failure.

And let's face it: No one likes to be "turned down." It can be tough on the ego. If we present the gospel and someone says "no," we tend to take it personally. We think we have failed in our attempt.

But have we? Remember that Jesus shared His message with thousands, and many did not accept Him. He witnessed, but many people said "no." Was He a failure? Of course not. At the end of His earthly ministry He prayed to His heavenly Father, "I brought glory to you here on earth by doing *everything* you told me to" (John 17:4). He had succeeded because He had done what He was supposed to do.

From these facts about Christ's ministry, let me share a conclusion I drew in *Witnessing Without Fear:*

> Our heavenly Father asks no more of us than this: that we obey His command to "Go, and preach the gospel to every creature . . ." His command is not to "convert everyone." Jesus did not, and neither can we. But we can obey; we can spread the message to all who will listen and trust God with the results.[1]

Even though people said "no" to our Lord, He was successful in presenting the gospel because He was faithful in doing so. He spread the message with love and compassion, and left the results to God. His example gives us two key thoughts that can liberate us from the fear of failure.

First, *success in witnessing is simply taking the initiative to share Christ in the power of the Holy Spirit, and leaving the results to God.* We do not fail if we obey what God has commanded us to do. Obedience, born of love and compassion, is God's only measure of success. The results are up to Him.

Second, *failure in witnessing = failing to witness.* We fail in witnessing only if we disobey God's command to share His love in the power of the Holy Spirit.

These truths have helped thousands of Christians around the world to break free from the fear of failure and begin to share Christ as a regular way of life—motivated by love and obedience. I strongly recommend that every Christian who desires a more fruitful ministry memorize these two definitions and rehearse them in their minds whenever a witnessing opportunity becomes evident.

The Holy Spirit will fill you with courage! "For God has not given us a spirit of timidity, but of power and love and discipline."

Lack of Practical Know-how

Countless Christians hear repeatedly that they should "take Christ to the marketplace," but they never receive the practical training that will ease their fears and prepare them to share their faith with confidence. Their questions are common ones:

"What do I say?"

"How do I start a conversation about Jesus?"

"How do I handle questions and arguments?"

"How can I be sure the person understands?"

"How do I encourage a decision?"

In recent years, more and more pastors have recognized the need for hands-on evangelism training. Several excellent programs are available.

Thousands of churches and study groups are using *Witnessing Without Fear,* which guides the believer step-by-step through the process of conquering fear, praying for an unsaved relative or friend, guiding a conversation toward Jesus, knowing what to say, handling questions and hostility, and following up a new Christian. Each chapter offers true-life stories and group discussion/action questions. We have received scores of reports from both laypersons and pastors indicating that their confidence and effectiveness in witnessing has increased dramatically after reading this book.

Campus Crusade also has produced an exciting new six-lesson video training package titled *Reaching Your World.* It includes attention-holding video vignettes and instruction, student workbooks, and a thorough leader's guide. (See Appendix E for information on how to obtain the resources mentioned in this chapter.)

Marcie was among the millions of believers who know they should share their faith but who are reluctant to try because they don't know what to say. Then she attended an evangelism training conference sponsored by several churches in her city.

Within just a couple of hours, she learned how to present Jesus Christ to others courteously and effectively through a little gospel presentation booklet called *The Four Spiritual Laws.* "At first I thought the booklet was too simple," she says, "and that our message must be more profound and complete than the message contained in the booklet. But as we went through the presentation together, I realized that it covers all the essential things a person needs to know in order to make a decision for Christ.

"Of course I was nervous the first few times I actually used my training. But the Holy Spirit reminded me that successful witnessing is simply taking the initiative to share Christ in the power of the Holy Spirit and leaving the results to God. The training I had received helped me communicate clearly, and I have had the blessing of seeing several people receive Christ!"

Recently Marcie has also used another booklet which Campus Crusade produces, *Would You Like to Know God Personally?* If she feels an individual might be more comfortable with this approach, she uses it instead of the *Four Spiritual Laws* booklet. Each contains the same basic message, but *Would You Like to Know God Personally?* has been slightly rephrased to appeal to one's felt need of a personal relationship with the God he has heard about all his life.

The practical know-how is available, and the Holy Spirit will help you put it to work!

The Missing Key to Happiness?

J. Stuart Holden wrote that "God does not invest a man with power for any other work than that of the Kingdom." I agree with him. Jesus promised that we would receive power when the Holy Spirit comes upon us, but in the same sentence He revealed what that power is for: that we be His witnesses. If we fail to exercise the discipline-privilege of witnessing for Him, we disobey His command and misappropriate the Holy Spirit's power.

My fellow Christians, we can study our Bibles until the Lord's return, attend church faithfully and pray diligently, know how to keep Christ on the throne and how to breathe spiritually, and partake of all God's other discipline-privileges—but if we disregard His wishes in this one area alone, we are disobedient. It is n t ours to choose which of His commands we will obey, for complete obedience is His only measure: "The one who obeys me is the one who loves me" (John 14:21).

I have stated this earlier, but it bears repeating at this crucial point: *It is absolutely impossible to be a happy, disobedient Christian.* One contradicts the other. When we disobey, we sin. By choosing to sin, we usurp the throne of our lives and are left unfulfilled, guilty and miserable.

But when we obey God's command to actively share His love, Christ remains on the throne! The way is clear for the Holy Spirit's love, joy, peace, patience, kindness, goodness, faithfulness, gentleness and self-control. Then, we find, *it is absolutely impossible to be a miserable, OBEDIENT Christian!*

The Fields Are Ripe

Never before in the history of this planet have so many individuals searched more openly for a sense of true significance. Men and women are longing for love, purpose, and knowledge of the one true God. While their searches take them in many directions such as materialism, humanism, the New Age movement or any of the thousands of false religions, we have in our possession the greatest gift to mankind—news of how men and women can join the family of God for eternity.

Two thousand years ago Jesus said, "The fields are ripe unto harvest." Today the fields are even riper, even more ready for reaping. We cannot afford to be selfish with the gospel when so many are living and dying without Him. Our love for Christ compels us to take the initiative to share His love and forgiveness whenever we have the opportunity, with all who will listen.

Do you love your Lord Jesus Christ? Then obey Him. Do you love others? Then tell them how they can receive

Him. As you are continually filled with the Holy Spirit, He will fill you with love, compassion and courage. Your job is to share the message; His job is to convict and convert, in His perfect timing.

FOR REFLECTION, DISCUSSION AND ACTION

1. Is it the Christian's prerogative to determine which of our Lord's commands he wants to follow? Explain your answer in relation to Acts 1:8 and John 14:21-24.

2. Have you been hesitant to witness to others? What are some of the reasons? Be specific.

3. Based on your obedience to Christ's command to share your faith in Him with others, what conclusion do you think He would draw about your love for Him?

4. Up to this point in your life, how have you defined success in witnessing? Failure in witnessing? Have you allowed your definitions to prevent you from sharing Christ? Why?

5. Memorize the definitions of "success in witnessing" and "failure in witnessing" from this chapter. Explain how these definitions will help you be more confident when witnessing opportunities come along.

6. Can you think of at least two people with whom the Holy Spirit is leading you to share Christ? Begin today to pray for these individuals and watch for that opening to share what Jesus Christ means to you.

7. Commit today to obtaining training to help you know how to share your faith with confidence. See Appendix E for the resources recommended in this chapter.

---

1. Bill Bright, *Witnessing Without Fear* (San Bernardino, CA: Here's Life Publishers, 1987), p. 67.

Appendix A

Would You Like to Know God Personally?

The following four principles will help you discover how to know God personally and experience the abundant life He promised.

1 GOD **LOVES** YOU AND CREATED YOU TO KNOW HIM PERSONALLY.

(References contained in these pages should be read in context from the Bible whenever possible.)

God's Love

"For God so loved the world, that He gave His only begotten Son, that whoever believes in Him should not perish, but have eternal life" (John 3:16).

God's Plan

"Now this is eternal life: that they may know you, the only true God, and Jesus Christ, whom you have sent" (John 17:3, NIV).

What prevents us from knowing God personally?

2 MAN IS **SINFUL** AND **SEPARATED** FROM GOD, SO WE CANNOT KNOW HIM PERSONALLY OR EXPERIENCE HIS LOVE.

Man Is Sinful

"For all have sinned and fall short of the glory of God" (Romans 3:23).

Man was created to have fellowship with God; but, because of his stubborn self-will, he chose to go his own independent way, and fellowship with God was broken. This self-will, characterized by an attitude of active rebellion or passive indifference, is evidence of what the Bible calls sin.

Man Is Separated

"For the wages of sin is death" (spiritual separation from God) (Romans 6:23).

This diagram illustrates that God is holy and man is sinful. A great gulf separates the two. The arrows illustrate that man is continually trying to reach God and establish a personal relationship with Him through his own efforts, such as a good life, philosophy or religion.

The third principle explains the only way to bridge this gulf . . .

3 JESUS CHRIST IS GOD'S ONLY PROVISION FOR MAN'S SIN. THROUGH HIM ALONE WE CAN KNOW GOD PERSONALLY AND EXPERIENCE HIS LOVE.

He Died in Our Place

"But God demonstrates His own love toward us, in that while we were yet sinners, Christ died for us" (Romans 5:8).

He Rose From the Dead

"Christ died for our sins . . . He was buried . . . He was raised on the third day, according to the Scriptures . . . He appeared to Peter, then to the twelve. After that He appeared to more than five hundred" (1 Corinthians 15:3-6).

He Is the Only Way to God

"Jesus said to him, 'I am the way, and the truth, and the life; no one comes to the Father, but through Me' " (John 14:6).

This diagram illustrates that God has bridged the gulf which separates us from Him by sending His Son, Jesus Christ, to die on the cross in our place to pay the penalty for our sins.

It is not enough just to know these truths...

4 WE MUST INDIVIDUALLY RECEIVE JESUS CHRIST AS SAVIOR AND LORD; THEN WE CAN KNOW GOD PERSONALLY AND EXPERIENCE HIS LOVE.

We Must Receive Christ

"But as many as received Him, to them He gave the right to become children of God, even to those who believe in His name" (John 1:12).

We Receive Christ Through Faith

"For by grace you have been saved through faith; and that not of yourselves, it is the gift of God; not as a result of works, that no one should boast" (Ephesians 2:8,9).

When We Receive Christ, We Experience a New Birth. (Read John 3:1-8.)

We Receive Christ by Personal Invitation

(Christ is speaking): "Behold, I stand at the door and knock; if anyone hears My voice and opens the door, I will come in to him" (Revelation 3:20).

Receiving Christ involves turning to God from self (repentance) and trusting Christ to come into our lives to forgive our sins and to make us the kind of people He wants us to be. Just to agree intellectually that Jesus Christ is the Son of God and that He died on the cross for our sins is not enough. Nor is it enough to have an emotional experience. We receive Jesus Christ by faith, as an act of the will.

These two circles represent two kinds of lives:

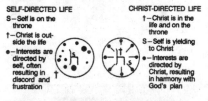

SELF-DIRECTED LIFE
S—Self is on the throne
†—Christ is outside the life
●—Interests are directed by self, often resulting in discord and frustration

CHRIST-DIRECTED LIFE
†—Christ is in the life and on the throne
S—Self is yielding to Christ
●—Interests are directed by Christ, resulting in harmony with God's plan

Which circle best represents your life? Which circle would you like to have represent your life?

The following explains how you can invite Jesus Christ into your life:

YOU CAN RECEIVE CHRIST RIGHT NOW BY FAITH THROUGH PRAYER

(Prayer is talking with God)

God knows your heart and is not so concerned with your words as He is with the attitude of your heart. The following is a suggested prayer:

> "Lord Jesus, I want to know You personally. Thank You for dying on the cross for my sins. I open the door of my life and receive You as my Savior and Lord. Thank You for forgiving my sins and giving me eternal life. Take control of the throne of my life. Make me the kind of person You want me to be."

Does this prayer express the desire of your heart?

If it does, pray this prayer right now, and Christ will come into your life, as He promised.

How to Know That Christ Is in Your Life

Did you receive Christ into your life? According to His promise in Revelation 3:20, where is Christ right now in relation to you? Christ said that He would come into your life and be your friend so you can know Him personally. Would He mislead you? On what authority do you know that God has answered your prayer? (The trustworthiness of God Himself and His Word.)

The Bible Promises Eternal Life to All Who Receive Christ

"And the witness is this, that God has given us eternal life, and this life is in His Son. He who has the Son has the life; he who does not have the Son of God does not have the life. These things I have written to you who believe in the name of the Son of God, in order that you may know that you have eternal life" (1 John 5:11-13).

Thank God often that Christ is in your life and that He will never leave you (Hebrews 13:5). You can know on the basis of His promise that Christ lives in you and that you have eternal life, from the very moment you invite Him in. He will not deceive you.

An important reminder . . .

DO NOT DEPEND ON FEELINGS

The promise of God's Word, the Bible—not our feelings—is our authority. The Christian lives by faith (trust) in the trustworthiness of God Himself and His Word. This train diagram illustrates the relationship between fact (God and His Word), faith (our trust in God and His Word), and feeling (the result of our faith and obedience) (John 14:21).

The train will run with or without the caboose. However, it would be useless to attempt to pull the train by the caboose. In the same way, we, as Christians, do not depend on feelings or emotions, but we place our faith (trust) in the trustworthiness of God and the promises of His Word.

Fellowship in a Good Church

God's Word admonishes us not to forsake "the assembling of ourselves together" (Hebrews 10:25). Several logs burn brightly together, but put one aside on the cold hearth and the fire goes out. So it is with your relationship with other Christians. If you do not belong to a church, do not wait to be invited. Take the initiative; call the pastor of a nearby church where Christ is honored and His Word is preached. Start this week, and make plans to attend regularly.

Suggestions for Christian Growth

Spiritual growth results from trusting Jesus Christ. "The righteous man shall live by faith" (Galatians 3:11). A life of faith will enable you to trust God increasingly with every detail of your life.

* * * * *

Appendix B

Have You Made the Wonderful Discovery?

Appendix B is an adaptation of the popular Campus Crusade for Christ booklet designed to help Christians share with other believers the joy of Spirit-controlled living. You may obtain copies of this booklet at Christian bookstores or directly from the publisher. See Appendix E for further information.

EVERY DAY CAN BE AN EXCITING ADVENTURE FOR THE CHRISTIAN who knows the reality of being filled with the Holy Spirit and who lives constantly, moment by moment, under His gracious direction.

The Bible tells us that there are three kinds of people:

1. NATURAL MAN

(One who has not received Christ)

"But a natural man does not accept the things of the Spirit of God; for they are foolishness to him, and he cannot understand them, because they are spiritually appraised" (1 Corinthians 2:14).

SELF-DIRECTED LIFE

S - Ego or finite self is on the throne
† - Christ is outside the life
• - Interests are directed by self, often resulting in discord and frustration

2. SPIRITUAL MAN

(One who is directed and empowered by the Holy Spirit)

"But he who is spiritual appraises all things" (1 Corinthians 2:15).

CHRIST-DIRECTED LIFE

† - Christ is in the life and on the throne
S - Self is yielding to Christ
• - Interests are directed by Christ, resulting in harmony with God's plan

3. CARNAL MAN

(One who has received Christ, but who lives in defeat because he trusts in his own efforts to live the Christian life)

"And I, brethren, could not speak to you as to spiritual men, but as to carnal men, as to babes in Christ. I gave you milk to drink, not solid food; for you were not yet able to receive it. Indeed, even now you are not yet able, for you are still carnal. For since there is jealousy and strife among you, are you not fleshly, and are you not walking like mere men?" (1 Corinthians 3:1-3)

SELF-DIRECTED LIFE

S - Self is on the throne
† - Christ dethroned and not allowed to direct the life
• - Interests are directed by self, often resulting in discord and frustration

1 GOD HAS PROVIDED FOR US AN ABUNDANT AND FRUITFUL CHRISTIAN LIFE.

Jesus said, "I came that they might have life, and might have it abundantly" (John 10:10).

"I am the vine, you are the branches; he who abides in Me, and I in him, he bears much fruit; for apart from Me you can do nothing" (John 15:5).

"But the fruit of the Spirit is love, joy, peace, patience, kindness, goodness, faithfulness, gentleness, self-control; against such things there is no law" (Galatians 5:22,23).

"But you shall receive power when the Holy Spirit has come upon you; and you shall be My witnesses both in Jerusalem, and in all Judea and Samaria, and even to the remotest part of the earth" (Acts 1:8).

THE SPIRITUAL MAN — Some personal traits which result from trusting God:

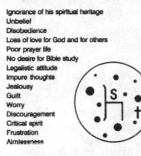

Christ-centered
Empowered by the Holy Spirit
Introduces others to Christ
Effective prayer life
Understands God's Word
Trusts God
Obeys God
Love
Joy
Peace
Patience
Kindness
Faithfulness
Goodness

The degree to which these traits are manifested in the life depends upon the extent to which the Christian trusts the Lord with every detail of his life, and upon his maturity in Christ. One who is only beginning to understand the ministry of the Holy Spirit should not be discouraged if he is not as fruitful as more mature Christians who have known and experienced this truth for a longer period.

Why is it that most Christians are not experiencing the abundant life?

2 **CARNAL CHRISTIANS CANNOT EXPERIENCE THE ABUNDANT AND FRUITFUL CHRISTIAN LIFE.**

The carnal man trusts in his own efforts to live the Christian life:

A. He is either uninformed about, or has forgotten, God's love, forgiveness and power (Romans 5:8-10; Hebrews 10:1-25; 1 John 1; 2:1-3; 2 Peter 1:9; Acts 1:8).

B. He has an up-and-down spiritual experience.

C. He cannot understand himself — he wants to do what is right, but cannot.

D. He fails to draw upon the power of the Holy Spirit to live the Christian life (1 Corinthians 3:1-3; Romans 7:15-24; 8:7; Galatians 5:16-18).

THE CARNAL MAN — Some or all of the following traits may characterize the Christian who does not fully trust God:

Ignorance of his spiritual heritage
Unbelief
Disobedience
Loss of love for God and for others
Poor prayer life
No desire for Bible study
Legalistic attitude
Impure thoughts
Jealousy
Guilt
Worry
Discouragement
Critical spirit
Frustration
Aimlessness

(The individual who professes to be a Christian but who continues to practice sin should realize that he may not be a Christian at all, according to 1 John 2:3; 3:6,9; Ephesians 5:5.)

The third truth gives us the only solution to this problem . . .

3 **JESUS PROMISED THE ABUNDANT AND FRUITFUL LIFE AS THE RESULT OF BEING FILLED (DIRECTED AND EMPOWERED) BY THE HOLY SPIRIT.**

The Spirit-filled life is the Christ-directed life by which Christ lives His life in and through us in the power of the Holy Spirit (John 15).

A. One becomes a Christian through the ministry of the Holy Spirit, according to John 3:1-8. From the moment of spiritual birth, the Christian is indwelt by the Holy Spirit at all times (John 1:12; Colossians 2:9,10; John 14:16,17).

Though all Christians are indwelt by the Holy Spirit, not all Christians are filled (directed and empowered) by the Holy Spirit on an ongoing basis.

B. The Holy Spirit is the source of the overflowing life (John 7:37-39).

C. The Holy Spirit came to glorify Christ (John 16:1-15). When one is filled with the Holy Spirit, he is a true disciple of Christ.

D. In His last command before His ascension, Christ promised the power of the Holy Spirit to enable us to be witnesses for Him (Acts 1:1-9).

How, then, can one be filled with the Holy Spirit?

4 WE ARE FILLED (DIRECTED AND EMPOWERED) BY THE HOLY SPIRIT BY FAITH; THEN WE CAN EXPERIENCE THE ABUNDANT AND FRUITFUL LIFE WHICH CHRIST PROMISED TO EACH CHRISTIAN.

You can appropriate the filling of the Holy Spirit **right now** if you:

A. Sincerely desire to be directed and empowered by the Holy Spirit (Matthew 5:6; John 7:37-39).

B. Confess your sins. By **faith** thank God that He **has** forgiven all of your sins—past, present and future—because Christ died for you (Colossians 2:13-15; 1 John 1; 2:1-3; Hebrews 10:1-17).

C. Present every area of your life to God (Romans 12:1,2).

D. By **faith** claim the fullness of the Holy Spirit, according to:

1. HIS COMMAND—Be filled with the Spirit. "And do not get drunk with wine, for that is dissipation, but be filled with the Spirit" (Ephesians 5:18).

2. HIS PROMISE—He will always answer when we pray according to His will. "And this is the confidence which we have before Him, that, if we ask any-thing according to His will, He hears us. And if we know that He hears us in whatever we ask, we know that we have the requests which we have asked from Him" (1 John 5:14,15).

Faith can be expressed through prayer...

How to Pray in Faith to be Filled With the Holy Spirit

We are filled with the Holy Spirit by **faith** alone. However, true prayer is one way of expressing your faith. The following is a suggested prayer:

"Dear Father, I need You. I acknowledge that I have been directing my own life and that, as a result, I have sinned against You. I thank You that You have forgiven my sins through Christ's death on the cross for me. I now invite Christ to again take His place on the throne of my life. Fill me with the Holy Spirit as You **commanded** me to be filled, and as You **promised** in Your Word that You would do if I asked in faith. I pray this in the name of Jesus. As an expression of my faith, I now thank You for directing my life and for filling me with the Holy Spirit."

Does this prayer express the desire of your heart? If so, bow in prayer and trust God to fill you with the Holy Spirit **right now.**

How to Know That You Are Filled (Directed and Empowered) by the Holy Spirit

Did you ask God to fill you with the Holy Spirit? Do you know that you are now filled with the Holy Spirit? On what authority? (On the trustworthiness of God Himself and His Word: Hebrews 11:6; Romans 14:22,23.)

Do not depend upon feelings. The promise of God's Word, not our feelings, is our authority. The Christian lives by faith (trust) in the trustworthiness of God Himself and His Word.

This train diagram illustrates the relationship between **fact** (God and His Word), **faith** (our trust in God and His Word), and **feeling** (the result of our faith and obedience) (John 14:21).

The train will run with or without the caboose. However, it would be futile to attempt to pull the train by the caboose. In the same way, we, as Christians, do not depend upon feelings or emotions, but we place our faith (trust) in the trustworthiness of God and the promises of His Word.

How to Walk in the Spirit

Faith (trust in God and in His promises) is the only means by which a Christian can live the Spirit-directed life. As you continue to trust Christ moment by moment:

A. Your life will demonstrate more and more of the fruit of the Spirit (Galatians 5:22,23) and will be more and more conformed to the image of Christ (Romans 12:2; 2 Corinthians 3:18).

B. Your prayer life and study of God's Word will become more meaningful.

C. You will experience His power in witnessing (Acts 1:8).

D. You will be prepared for spiritual conflict against the world (1 John 2:15-17); against the flesh (Galatians 5:16,17); and against Satan (1 Peter 5:7-9; Ephesians 6:10-13).

E. You will experience His power to resist temptation and sin (1 Corinthians 10:13; Philippians 4:13; Ephesians 1:19-23; 6:10; 2 Timothy 1:7; Romans 6:1-16).

Spiritual Breathing

By faith you can continue to experience God's love and forgiveness.

If you become aware of an area of your life (an attitude or an action) that is displeasing to the Lord, even though you are walking with Him and sincerely desiring to serve Him, simply thank God that He has forgiven your sins — past, present and future — on the basis of Christ's death on the cross. Claim His love and forgiveness by faith and continue to have fellowship with Him.

If you retake the throne of your life through sin — a definite act of disobedience — breathe spiritually.

Spiritual Breathing (exhaling the impure and inhaling the pure) is an exercise in faith and enables you to continue to experience God's love and forgiveness.

1. **Exhale** — confess your sin — agree with God concerning your sin and thank Him for His forgiveness of it, according to 1 John 1:9 and Hebrews 10:1-25. Confession involves repentance — a change in attitude and action.

2. **Inhale** — surrender the control of your life to Christ, and appropriate (receive) the fullness of the Holy Spirit by faith. Trust that He now directs and empowers you, according to the **command** of Ephesians 5:18 and the **promise** of 1 John 5:14,15.

Appendix C

Spiritual Gifts Defined

Following are general definitions of gifts of the Holy Spirit which are mentioned in the passages found in 1 Corinthians 12 and 14, Romans 12 and Ephesians 4:

Wisdom (1 Corinthians 12:8)

Wisdom is a natural ability that is generally developed over a long period of time by all people. The spiritual gift of wisdom, however, while usually acquired as the believer matures spiritually, can also be instantaneous in nature. That is to say that a Christian who has this gift can clearly discern the mind of Christ in applying specific knowledge to specific needs that arise within the body of Christ.

Knowledge (1 Corinthians 12:8)

Knowledge is another spiritual gift that has a counterpart in natural talent. Everyone is born with the natural ability to discover certain information and formulate ideas from that information. But the Christian who has the spiritual gift of knowledge has a supernatural ability to discover, accumulate, analyze and clarify information and ideas that are pertinent to the growth and well-being of the body of Christ.

Faith (1 Corinthians 12:9)

All believers are given faith in some measure and for certain reasons. For example, every believer is given the ability to have faith in Christ for his salvation. Each Christian is also to live by faith. Beyond that, faith is a spiritual gift that the believer may develop and apply in virtually every area of life.

This gift is the special ability to discern with extraordinary confidence the will and purposes of God as they relate to the growth and well-being of the body of Christ. It is evident in the lives of those ministers and laymen who do believe, as contrasted with the lives of those who do not.

Healing (1 Corinthians 12:8,28)

The gift of healing does not suggest that the recipient of the gift is given supernatural powers over the human body and over disease. Rather, it means that the individual is given the privilege of being the vessel through whom God's works of healing are directed.

Healing in a strict sense is a miracle of God. This gift is available in its application to all Christians through the ministry of the elders of the church. This is described in James 5:14,15:

> Is anyone sick? He should call for the elders of the church and they should pray over him and pour a little oil upon him, calling on the Lord to heal him. And their prayer, if offered in faith, will heal him, for the Lord will make him well; and if his sickness was caused by some sin, the Lord will forgive him (TLB).

Doctors and others in the medical profession may acquire certain skills and develop certain natural abilities in the areas of medicine, but the healing itself is a miraculous wonder of the life process which is uniquely controlled by God. Many Christian doctors have natural and acquired abilities which are complemented by the gift of healing.

Miracles (1 Corinthians 12:10,28)

The gift of miracles is the supernatural ability given to certain believers through whom the Holy Spirit performs acts by means outside the ordinary laws of nature.

The Bible contains many illustrations of miracles, many of them performed by the Lord Himself. And, in Revelation 11, we read that at some future time believers will be given miraculous powers through the indwelling of the Holy Spirit. Nowhere in Scripture do we read that the granting of this very special gift has been temporarily held back by the Holy Spirit.

Prophecy (1 Corinthians 12:10,28)

The gift of prophecy is one of the most misunderstood of all the gifts. Many people consider it the ability to foretell the future. The word literally means to "preach" or to proclaim the Word of God to others. A prophet, biblically, called a nation to repentance and to a return to God. Most believers who have this gift find that it takes much time, hard work and reliance on the power and control of the Holy Spirit to develop this gift.

Since so much of Scripture contains God's revelation of His future plans, the preaching of the Word from time to time includes dealing with things to come. Since the canon of Scripture is now "closed," or complete, such preaching on future things, if it is the result of being truly gifted, only confirms what the Bible says and does not add to the Scriptures.

Discerning of Spirits (1 Corinthians 12:10)

The gift of discerning of spirits is the supernatural ability of certain believers to discern whether things said and done by others are true or false, are of God or of Satan, are of the Holy Spirit or of the flesh. The writer of the book of Hebrews tells us, "You will never be able to eat solid spiritual food and understand the deeper things of God's Word until you become better Christians and learn right from wrong by practicing doing right" (Hebrews 5:14, TLB).

This passage indicates to us that discernment of spirits is an ability which is learned over a period of time.

Tongues (1 Corinthians 12:10,28)

The gift of tongues is the supernatural ability to speak to others and/or to God in a language or utterance never learned by the speaker. Like all the other gifts of the Holy Spirit, the gift of tongues has been given to the Church in order to glorify Christ and to build up the body of Christ (1 Corinthians 14:26). Unhappily, however, tongues has often become a divisive issue among all too many Christians.

Many others have written extensively (and exhaustively) on the "issue" of tongues, and it is doubtful that much could be written here that has not already been stated. Let me stress only two biblical principles: First, the gift of tongues must always be exercised in accordance with the biblical guidelines as mentioned in 1 Corinthians 14. Second, those who have this gift must exercise it in love and humility, and those who do not have this gift must accept with love those who claim to have it.

We must aim for equality and not sameness among the members of the body of Christ (2 Corinthians 8:14). And in so doing, we must seek first to glorify Christ and then to build up one another toward unity in the Holy Spirit. I suggest that you read again and again the passage of Scripture found in 1 Peter 4:7-19.

Interpretation of Tongues (1 Corinthians 14:13)

The gift of tongues may or may not be accompanied by the giving of another closely related gift, the interpretation of tongues. Whenever the gift of tongues is exercised in the presence of others, the person speaking in tongues is to "pray also for the gift of knowing what he has said, so that he can tell people afterwards, plainly" (1 Corinthians 14:13, TLB).

Apostleship (1 Corinthians 14:28; Ephesians 4:11)

Some Christians are given special abilities with which to perform the functions of the office of the Church that is termed *apostle*. Thus the gift of apostleship. It was granted to the original 12 apostles, then others after them, including Paul (Acts 1:26; Romans 1:1; Acts 14:14; Romans 16:7; 1 Thessalonians 2:6).

Though we do not have people who could claim to be apostles in the original sense—those who had been eyewitnesses of the resurrected Christ (Acts 21:26)—today we would have those who may function much like an apostle. In a general sense, then, an apostle is one who is gifted by the Holy Spirit with the special ability to give leadership to a number of churches and to show supernatural wisdom and authority in spiritual matters that relate to those churches.

Teaching (1 Corinthians 12:28; Romans 12:7; Ephesians 4:11)

The gift of teaching is the supernatural ability to explain information to members of the Body of Christ in such a way that they will be edified and able readily to apply it in their lives. This gift develops with maturity.

Teaching is a very common natural talent. But not all natural teaching is beneficial. Only the spiritual gift of teaching can bring about righteous results in the lives of others. This is true for two reasons:

First, the Christian's ability to teach is supernaturally imparted by the Holy Spirit. Since God is holy, therefore, any gift of His would be holy and could not be used in an unholy fashion, if properly exercised in the power and control of the Holy Spirit.

Second, for the Christian, the gift of teaching is the supernatural ability to teach *truths*. Since all truth is ultimately from God, it can have only a beneficial impact on the life of the student when properly applied.

Helps, Service and Mercy (1 Corinthians 12:28; Romans 12:7,8; Ephesians 4:12)

The spiritual gifts of helps, service and mercy are similar in many respects. All three are given for the building up of the body of Christ, but they differ slightly.

The gift of helps is characteristically more *task*-oriented. The gift of service is more *people*-oriented. The gift of mercy is extended usually to the infirm, the elderly or the injured, who are unable to totally care for themselves.

Administration (1 Corinthians 11:28)

The gift of administration (called "governments" in some translations of the Bible) is the special ability given by the Holy Spirit to some believers enabling them to understand the objectives of a particular group within the Body of Christ and to make and carry out plans for realizing those objectives.

We sometimes confuse this spiritual gift with the gift of leadership. While some leaders might also have the gift of administration, all do not. Conversely, not all who have the gift of administration have the gift of leadership.

Leadership (Romans 12:8)

The spiritual gift of leadership is the special ability given by the Holy Spirit to certain members of the Body of Christ for the purpose of setting goals and motivating and directing the activities of others in working together toward accomplishing those goals.

An individual who has the gift of leadership but not of administration would do well to have supportive staff who are gifted in administration. Otherwise, and we see this too often, a leader will emerge who will establish goals and highly motivate people to work together to reach those goals only to fail because of poor planning, organization, direction and controls.

Likewise, a well-organized local church which lacks a leader may flounder from misdirection or stagnancy, and its people may become frustrated and unfulfilled because of the slow rate or lack of progress in the life and growth of the church.

Exhortation (1 Corinthians 12:10)

The gift of exhortation is the special ability given by the Holy Spirit to certain members of the Body of Christ to minister to groups or to individuals, on a short-term basis, words of comfort, consolation, encouragement and counsel. The result of such counseling to other members of the body of Christ is that those exhorted will feel helped and healed.

Another term for exhortation would be to "build up" one another in Christ. Hebrews 3:13 tells us to do just that: "Exhort one another daily." Each of us is told to exercise this special ability, and therefore each of us, as Christians, is assured that the Holy Spirit will empower us with this gift: "For I can do everything God asks me to with the help of Christ who gives me the strength and power" (Philippians 4:13, TLB).

Giving (Romans 12:8)

In my many years with the ministry of Campus Crusade for

Christ, I have seen the gift of giving demonstrated over and over again. This gift is the supernatural ability to acquire money for the purpose of giving it to others for the sole purpose of carrying out the work of God.

Those who posses this gift are among the happiest and most cheerful people I know. This is proof of the Lord's promise, "It is more blessed to give than to receive" (Acts 20:35, TLB). We cannot outgive God. "Give, and it will be given to you" (Luke 6:38, NASB).

Evangelism (Ephesians 4:11)

Ephesians 4:11 refers to evangelism as an office; however, I believe it is also a special ability given by the Holy Spirit to certain believers, though granted in different and varying amounts. While some are given this special ability, the Bible teaches that the Church is commissioned to preach the gospel throughout the world (Matthew 28:19,20), and that the Lord promised that the Holy Spirit would indwell all believers for the specific purpose of witnessing for Him (Acts 1:8).

Out of love for the Lord and in obedience to His command, all believers are to be witnesses for Him as a way of life. The supernaturalness of this gift lies in our motivation that is prompted by the Holy Spirit to want to share Christ, and in the power of the Holy Spirit to open minds to the gospel when it is shared. All Christians should share Christ with others. Those who are more gifted in evangelism should devote even more time to seeking to reach others for Christ.

Pastoring (Ephesians 4:11)

The office of pastor, as listed in Ephesians 4, indicates that certain members of the body of Christ are given special abilities by the Holy Spirit to pastor or "shepherd" the members of that unit of the Church. This gift gives one the ability to care for the interests of those believers whom God has committed to that person's care.

The gift of pastoring, however, is not limited to those who hold the church office of pastor. A lay person who has a strong desire to disciple or shepherd a group of people in his home may

well have the gift of pastoring. All too often the entire respon-
sibility of pastoring in a local church is limited to the office of
pastor. Among the most dynamic local churches I have seen are
those in which the gift of pastoring is recognized among the laity
and its practice encouraged.

Total Availability to God

As we have seen in this appendix, many of the spiritual gifts
are similar in nature, and many times individuals may have two
or more gifts that greatly complement one another. Again, I want
to say that knowing what our spiritual gifts are is much less important than being available to God at all times and in every way
to build up the Body of Christ.

Remember too that spiritual gifts are not a mark of
spirituality. That was obvious in the Corinthian church, one of
the most carnal churches of all, and yet one in which there was
a wrongly motivated overemphasis on spiritual gifts.

Finally, we can know that we are living Spirit-filled lives,
not by the manifestation of spiritual gifts, but when the fruit of
the Spirit, which is primarily love, becomes increasingly evident
in our lives.

*Adapted by permission from THE HOLY SPIRIT: THE KEY TO SUPER-
NATURAL LIVING by Bill Bright (Here's Life Publishers, 1980).*

Appendix D

How to Help Change Your World

"*I sense God's hand on this most important endeavor. God's people are coming together. So many different denominations and mission agencies are answering Christ's call to unite and get the Good News out quickly. I count it a rare privilege to be involved closely with New Life 2000.*"

Dr. Ted Engstrom
President Emeritus, World Vision
Chairman, New Life 2000
Committee of Reference

One of the most exciting aspects of the Spirit-directed walk is that we have the matchless privilege and opportunity of helping share the Good News with our world. Have you ever seriously considered how you can help change the world for the glory of God?

Right now, thousands of Christian organizations and churches are teaming up for a comprehensive, ongoing thrust into all regions of the globe to help share God's love and forgiveness with those who do not know Him. The strategy involves millions of obedient Christians from all walks of life—and you can be one of them!

What is New Life 2000?

New Life 2000 is a comprehensive plan for world evangelism—a strategy to help fulfill the Great Commission in obedience to our Lord's command in Matthew 28:18-20. Through this plan every Christian can play a significant role in helping to take the message of new life in Jesus Christ to the entire world by the year 2000.

New Life 2000 links the almost forty years of evangelism and discipleship training of Campus Crusade for Christ with millions of Christians from thousands of churches of all denominations and other Christian ministries, which are committed to helping fulfill the Great Commission.

The strategy of New Life 2000 includes establishing 5,000 ministry areas throughout the world— one center for each population area of approximately one million people. A New Life Training Center, with its tailor-made, culturalized ministry strategy, will be located in each area.

Each New Life Training Center, directed by local national Christians, will coordinate the work of evangelism and discipleship as part of a comprehensive outreach strategy in its area. The strategy includes the use of the "JESUS" film and an ongoing leadership training program, which emphasizes "spiritual multiplication" in accordance with 2 Timothy 2:2.

Within each of the 5,000 areas, we anticipate planting hundreds of New Life Groups, ranging in size from 10 to 30 people, composed largely of new Christians. The groups meet one or more times each week to teach believers the biblical basis for a vital Christian walk and fruitful ministry. In many areas, New Life Groups cluster to form new churches in alliance with existing local churches of various denominations.

(The cost for a New Life Training Center, including staff salaries, equipment, transportation, etc. will average $50,000 per year. Depending on country and culture, the cost will range from $30,000 to $70,000. After three to five years, the centers should be self-supporting by national believers.)

Why is Campus Crusade for Christ launching New Life 2000?

Trained Christians reaching others with the gospel in their own language in every community worldwide, has been at the heart of Campus Crusade for Christ since the ministry began in 1951.

New Life 2000 is not a new plan. It is an acceleration of Campus Crusade's nearly four decades of serving the body of

believers, helping them "go and preach the gospel to every crea-
ture" and helping new Christians to grow in their personal
relationship with God, so that they will, in turn, win and disciple
others, generation after generation, through the process of
spiritual multiplication.

What are the goals of New Life 2000?

- Present the gospel to more than 6 billion people by
  the year 2000.
- Introduce at least 1 billion people to faith in Jesus
  Christ.
- Involve 200 million new Christians in New Life
  Groups.
- Train millions of leaders through 5,000 New Life
  Training Centers.
- Establish discipleship and training ministries on
  8,000 campuses worldwide to help introduce mil-
  lions of college students and their professors to
  Christ.
- Start 10 million New Life Groups.
- Help establish more than 1 million churches in
  cooperation with thousands of churches of all
  denominations.
- Assist local churches and individuals in adopting
  one or more of the 5,000 New Life Training Centers
  at an average cost of $50,000 per center.

Who is involved in New Life 2000?

Christians from North America, Europe and more than 150
nations around the world are a part of New Life 2000. These men
and women from diverse backgrounds include pastors, students,
businessmen, homemakers, diplomats, prisoners, farmers, ath-
letes, executives and military leaders.

Millions of believers within thousands of churches,
denominations, organizations and mission agencies are uniting
to make New Life 2000 a priority for their evangelism and dis-

cipleship ministries at home and abroad.

The "JESUS" Film

The "JESUS" film, sponsored and financed through Campus Crusade for Christ, and filmed in Israel, is believed to be the most biblically accurate feature motion picture on the life of our Lord Jesus Christ ever produced.

By January 1, 1989, it had been viewed by approximately 330 million people in live audiences, in 128 languages, with 47 languages in process. Tens of millions have already indicated salvation decisions for Christ. The goal of New Life 2000 is to make the "JESUS" film available in 300 major languages, representing every language group of a million or more people, and at least 1,000 dialects.

We are praying for and believing God that more than 1 billion people will be introduced to Christ through this film ministry along with the many other evangelistic efforts of New Life 2000. The film is also effective among students, executives and other specialized groups in North America, as well as among hidden people in Third World countries.

Many churches in North America will be training their members to show the "JESUS" film evangelistically in their homes. For example, Dr. Jack Hayford, pastor of Church on the Way, Van Nuys, California, and his associates are training 1,000 couples to show the "JESUS" film in their homes at least twice each year. They are anticipating that at least 1,000 to 2,000 people will be reached for Christ through this and other evangelistic efforts in their church this year.

Today through New Life 2000, you can know with absolute assurance that your life has counted . . . that you have helped to lead millions of people into Christ's kingdom.

Will you dare to believe God that your partnership in New Life 2000 could help bring the message of Jesus Christ to the whole world by the end of this century?

"It has been my privilege to know Bill Bright and the ministry of Campus Crusade for Christ for nearly 40 years, and for that and other reasons I am happy to serve as honorary chairman of New Life 2000.

"I believe that it is going to be an enterprise that can help touch the entire world for Christ by the end of this century. We are going to be praying and working together, and I hope that you and your church will get behind it and make this one of the greatest evangelistic efforts in the history of the church in modern times."

Dr. Billy Graham
Evangelist
Honorary Chairman, New Life 2000

For more information on how you can be a part of this vital strategy, please write:

Campus Crusade for Christ
Office of Communications (41-50)
Arrowhead Springs
San Bernardino, CA 92414

New Life 2000 is a service mark of Campus Crusade for Christ International.

Appendix E

Resources to Help You Grow and Share the Good News

For Personal Evangelism

Have You Heard of the Four Spiritual Laws? *Bill Bright.* One of the most effective and widely used evangelistic tools ever developed, the Four Spiritual Laws gives you a meaningful, easy-to-use way of sharing your faith with others. 0-86605-064-7/Pkg. of 50

Would You Like to Know God Personally? A new adaptation of the Four Spiritual Laws, presented as four principles for establishing a personal relationship with God through Jesus Christ. 0-89840-204-2/Pkg. of 50

Witnessing Without Fear. *Bill Bright,* with a foreword by Billy Graham. A step-by-step guide to sharing your faith with confidence. "The chapter on 'Conquering the Fear of Failure' is worth the price of the book," says Ann Kiemel Anderson. Pastor Charles Stanley writes, "If you're praying for an unbelieving friend, neighbor or loved one, this book is for you." Ideal for both individual and group study; a Gold Medallion Award winner. 0-89840-176-3

Reaching Your World. A six-part video/workbook package for Sunday school classes, midweek Bible studies, and visitation or evangelism training. Includes video vignettes and instruction, student workbooks, leader's guide, copies of *Witnessing Without Fear* and evangelistic booklets.

Jesus and the Intellectual. *Bill Bright.* Investigates the claims of Christ and the validity of Christianity from an intellec-

199

tual and felt-need point of view. *Jesus and the Intellectual* includes Bible verses and a four-point outline of the gospel. It's a useful evangelistic and follow-up tool. 0-86605-071-X/Pkg. of 5

Good News Comic Book (Children). Introduce children to Christ with this colorful gospel story. Children can use it to share with other children. It's an excellent gift for birthdays or holidays. 0-86605-069-8/Pkg. of 25

How to Get Better Grades and Have More Fun (High School and College). *Steve Douglass and Al Janssen.* Here's what every student is looking for: help from a Harvard MBA for getting better grades and spending less time doing it. It gives practical guidance to help all students raise their grade point average, deal with stress and manage their time. Includes a clear presentation of the gospel. Fast reading and easy to apply. 0-89840-090-2

How to Achieve Your Potential and Enjoy Life (Adult). *Steve Douglass and Al Janssen.* Written by a Harvard MBA in the popular style of *How to Get Better Grades and Have More Fun,* this book helps adults who want to find success and fulfillment. Practical, motivational, and with a clear presentation of the gospel. An ideal book to share with your non-Christian friends. 0-89840-184-4

Tell It Often, Tell It Well. *Mark McCloskey.* You can gain confidence and practical help to initiate sharing your Christian faith with others through this motivating and insightful book. It is a well-reasoned, biblical approach to fruitful witnessing, and is used as a text in several Bible colleges and seminaries. 0-89840-124-0

For Personal Discipleship

Personal Disciplemaking. *Christopher B. Adsit.* A step-by-step guide for leading a Christian from new birth to maturity. Howard Hendricks writes, "This is the most comprehensive, practical approach to one-on-one disciplemaking I have seen." 0-89840-213-1

The First Year of Your Christian Life. *Steven L. Pogue.* Ideal for New Convert classes or for use as a personal gift for a new Christian, this book helps the new Christian understand the essential basics of his walk with Jesus Christ. 0-89840-195-X

Transferable Concepts. *Bill Bright.* These booklets explain the "how-to's" of consistent, successful Christian living. They're great for personal follow-up and discipleship. They are also available as one conveniently bound paperback titled *Transferable Concepts for Powerful Living.*

How to be Sure You Are a Christian
How to Experience God's Love and Forgiveness
How to be Filled With the Spirit
How to Walk in the Spirit
How to Pray
How to Witness in the Spirit
How to Introduce Others to Christ
How to Help Fulfill the Great Commission
How to Love by Faith
How to be an Effective Member of the Body of Christ

Five Steps to Christian Growth. Establishes new believers in five cornerstones of the faith: assurance of salvation, steps to growing, understanding God's love, experiencing God's forgiveness and being filled with the Spirit. 0-91856-33-101 *Leader's Guide*/0-918956-34-X

Ten Basic Steps Toward Christian Maturity. *Bill Bright.* These eleven individual booklets from the *Handbook for Christian Maturity* cover practical, biblical steps to developing your Christian walk.

Introduction — The Uniqueness of Jesus
Step 1 — The Christian Adventure
Step 2 — The Christian and the Abundant Life
Step 3 — The Christian and the Holy Spirit
Step 4 — The Christian and Prayer
Step 5 — The Christian and the Bible
Step 6 — The Christian and Obedience
Step 7 — The Christian and Witnessing
Step 8 — The Christian and Stewardship
Step 9 — Highlights of the Old Testament
Step 10 — Highlights of the New Testament

Transferable Concepts for Powerful Living. *Bill Bright.* This book will give you and your disciples the help you need for a consistent and victorious Christian walk. Previously available only as Transferable Concepts booklets, these lessons are now compiled into one convenient study guide. Discover the ten most important ingredients for enriching your spiritual life and learn ways to pass this vital information on to others. 0-86605-163-5 *Leader's Guide*/0-86605-161-9

Handbook for Christian Maturity. *Bill Bright.* As the follow-up material for the nationwide Power for Living campaign, this book has fostered new life and growth among individuals and study groups looking for help in understanding the Christian life. You'll focus on the ten most essential building blocks for developing a strong walk of faith. 0-86605-010-8

Knowing God's Heart, Sharing His Joy: A 31-Day Experiment. *Dick Purnell.* For all who would like to know and share what is on God's heart, Dick Purnell has prepared thirty-one days of personal Bible study, prayer and practical implementation. You'll discover the burden on God's heart for the world, and then move to the message God has for everyone, especially those who do not have a personal relationship with Christ. 0-89840-219-0

Promises: A Daily Guide to Supernatural Living. *Bill Bright.* A daily devotional guide to help change your life. Live a supernatural life every day by meditating and acting upon God's promises. Now available in paperback. 0-86605-178-3

At Christian bookstores everywhere.
Or call
Here's Life Publishers
1-800-854-5659
In California call (714) 886-7981